A Framework for Understanding Poverty

10 Actions to Educate Students

Workbook

Ruby K. Payne, Ph.D.

Payne, Ruby K., Ph.D.
A Framework for Understanding Poverty: 10 Actions to Educate Students workbook.
Fourth edition, 2012. Revised 2015

  100 pp.
  Bibliography pp. 91–92
  ISBN-13: 978-1-934583-62-3
  ISBN-10: 1-934583-62-6

1. Education   2. Sociology   3. Title

Other selected titles by Ruby K. Payne, Ph.D.

A Framework for Understanding Poverty
Under-Resourced Learners: 8 Strategies to Improve Student Achievement
Research-Based Strategies: Narrowing the Achievement Gap for Under-Resourced Learners
School Improvement: 9 Systemic Processes to Raise Achievement (Payne & Magee)
From Understanding Poverty to Building Human Capacity: Ruby Payne's Articles on
    Transforming Individuals, Families, Schools, Churches, and Communities
Un Marco Para Entender La Pobreza (Spanish edition of *Framework*)
Understanding Learning: the How, the Why, the What
Working with Parents: Building Relationships for Student Success
Working with Students: Discipline Strategies for the 21st-Century Classroom
Crossing the Tracks for Love: What to Do When You and Your Partner Grew Up in
    Different Worlds
Removing the Mask: Giftedness in Poverty (Slocumb & Payne)
Bridges Out of Poverty: Strategies for Professionals and Communities (Payne, DeVol, &
    Dreussi-Smith)
Think Rather of Zebra: Dealing with Aspects of Poverty Through Story (Stailey & Payne)
What Every Church Member Should Know About Poverty (Ehlig & Payne)
Living on a Tightrope: a Survival Handbook for Principals (Sommers & Payne)
Hidden Rules of Class at Work (Payne & Krabill)

Table of Contents

My Personal Experience with Class

NOTE: The purpose of this exercise is simply to illustrate that the broader a person's experience, the greater the potential understanding of different economic realities. There is no assigned value (good or bad) for any item.

Place a check next to each of the following that applies to you:

- ☐ have ever lived in a home larger than 10,000 square feet
- ☐ have ever lived in an inner city
- ☐ have ever traveled to a Third World country
- ☐ have ever lived in a trailer/mobile home
- ☐ have two friends who grew up in poverty
- ☐ have flown in an airplane
- ☐ have taken a vacation more than 50 miles from home and did not stay with a relative
- ☐ have had private music lessons
- ☐ have used public transportation to get to work or school
- ☐ have a member of your immediate family who is on disability
- ☐ know an adult who has never had a full-time job
- ☐ have been to a country club
- ☐ have been to a debutante event
- ☐ know the CEO of a company that has more than $30 million in revenue
- ☐ have been to a charity event and met a state governor or the president of the United States
- ☐ know someone personally who was killed in a drug- or gang-related incident
- ☐ have been inside a homeless shelter
- ☐ have a friend who was in foster care
- ☐ have friends or relatives who have not gone past the eighth grade
- ☐ have a friend or relative who has ever received food stamps or services from a free clinic
- ☐ know someone personally who has been in wealth for two generations or more
- ☐ can describe the difference between a trust fund and a will

What is this cognitive frame?

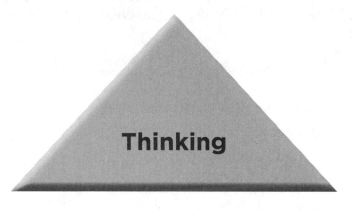

Relationships and knowledge

Thinking

Demands of environment

Resources

Continuum of Resources

Resources help build stability

UNDER-RESOURCED		RESOURCED
Instability/crisis	. . . .	Stability
Isolation	. . . .	Exposure
Dysfunction	. . . .	Functionality
Concrete reality	. . . .	Abstract, representational reality
Casual, oral language	. . . .	Written, formal register
Thought polarization	. . . .	Option seeking
Survival	. . . .	Abundance
No work/intermittent work	. . . .	Work/careers/larger cause
Poverty	. . . .	Wealth
Less educated	. . . .	More educated

Mental Model for Poverty

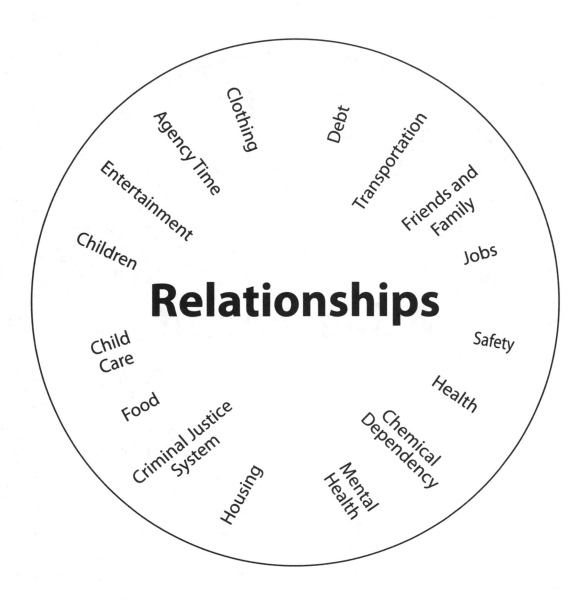

Actual responses from people living in poverty.

Note. Developed by Phil DeVol, 2006.

Mental Model for Middle Class

Achievement

Shopping

Hobbies/Sports

Transportation

Vacation

Family and Friends

Children's Activities

Clubs and Civic Groups/ Volunteering

Child Care

Health

Debt

Chemical Dependency

Careers

Mental Health

Political Action

Retirement

Prevention

Education

Note. Developed by Phil DeVol, 2006.

Mental Model for Wealth

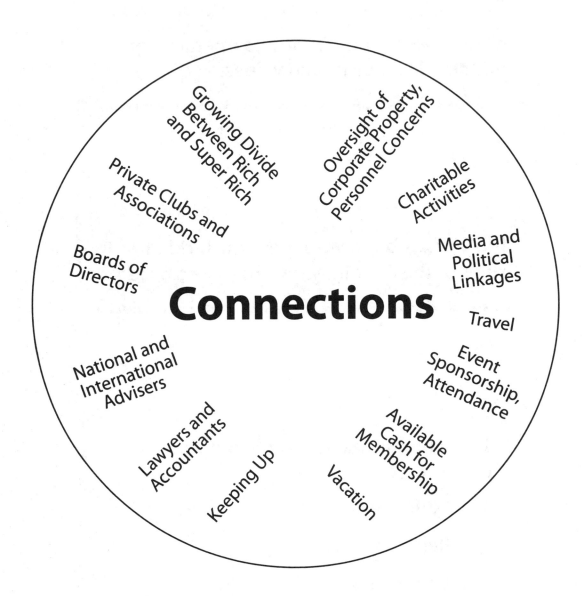

Growing Divide Between Rich and Super Rich

Private Clubs and Associations

Boards of Directors

National and International Advisers

Lawyers and Accountants

Keeping Up

Vacation

Available Cash for Membership

Event Sponsorship, Attendance

Travel

Media and Political Linkages

Charitable Activities

Oversight of Corporate Property, Personnel Concerns

Connections

Note. Developed by Ruby Payne, 2005.

Key Points

Most schools and businesses operate from middle-class norms and values.

Individuals bring with them the hidden rules of the class in which they were raised.

Three things that help one move out of poverty are:

- Education
- Relationships
- Employment

10 Actions to Educate Students

	Action	Why?	Page
1	Build relationships of mutual respect.	Motivation for learning.	8
2	Teach students the hidden rules of school.	Hidden rules break relationships, and without relationships learning is decreased.	14
3	Analyze the resources of your students, and make interventions based on resources the students have access to.	Interventions do not work if they are based on resources that are not available.	24
4	Teach formal register, the language of school and work.	To understand written text, which is essential for success at school and work.	36
5	Teach abstract processes.	All learning involves *what, why,* and *how.* The *how* piece must be direct-taught for tasks to be done.	39
6	Teach mental models.	Mental models translate between the abstract representational world and the sensory concrete world.	43
7	Teach students how to plan.	To control impulsivity for task completion.	46
8	Use the adult voice and reframing to change behaviors.	To maintain relationships and get the appropriate behaviors.	49
9	Understand the family resources and dynamics.	To better understand the resources the child has access to and better select interventions.	56
10	Teach how to ask questions.	So students can get past the third-grade reading level—and so they can get inside their head and know what they know and what they don't know.	61

10 Actions to Educate Students

1. Relationships

Build relationships of mutual respect.

Why?

Motivation for learning.

Key Points

To move from poverty to middle class, one must give up (for a period of time) relationships for achievement.

Four reasons one leaves poverty are:
- Too painful to stay
- Vision or goal
- Key relationship
- Special talent/skill

Relationships of mutual respect involve:
- Support
- High expectations
- Insistence

If a student and teacher do not have a relationship of mutual respect, the learning will be significantly reduced. For some students, it won't occur at all.

If a student and a teacher don't like each other—or even come to despise each other—forget about significant learning.

If mutual respect is present, it can compensate for the dislike.

Mutual respect is as much about nonverbals as it is about what you say.

Relationships of mutual respect must have three things present:

- Support: the direct-teaching of process and mental models.
- High expectations: the approach that says, "I know you can do it, and you will."
- Insistence: the motivation and persistence that come from the relationship.

For mutual respect to exist, there must be structure, consequence, and choice.

- Structure is the external parameters and internal boundaries.
- Consequence is what happens when structure is not honored.
- Choice is an individual decision regarding those parameters and boundaries.

Creating Relationships

DEPOSITS	WITHDRAWALS
Seeking first to understand	Seeking first to be understood
Keeping promises	Breaking promises
Kindnesses, courtesies	Unkindnesses, discourtesies
Clarifying expectations	Violating expectations
Loyalty to the absent	Disloyalty, duplicity
Apologies	Pride, conceit, arrogance
Open to feedback	Rejecting feedback

Note. Adapted from *The 7 Habits of Highly Effective People,* by Stephen Covey, 1989.

DEPOSITS MADE TO INDIVIDUAL IN POVERTY	WITHDRAWALS MADE FROM INDIVIDUAL IN POVERTY
Appreciation for humor and entertainment provided by the individual	Put-downs or sarcasm about the humor or the individual
Acceptance of what the individual cannot say about a person or situation	Insistence and demands for full explanation about a person or situation
Respect for the demands and priorities of relationships	Insistence on the middle-class view of relationships
Using the adult voice	Using the parent voice
Assisting with goal setting	Telling the individual his/her goals
Identifying options related to available resources	Making judgments based on the value and availability of resources
Understanding the importance of personal freedom, speech, and individual personality	Assigning pejorative character traits to the individual

What Can a Teacher Do to Build Relationships?

TESA (Teacher Expectations & Student Achievement) identified 15 behaviors that teachers use with good students.

The research study found that when teachers used these interactions with low-achieving students, their achievement made significant gains.

1. Calls on everyone in the room equitably.
2. Provides individual help.
3. Gives "wait" time (allows student enough time to answer).
4. Asks questions to give the student clues about the answer.
5. Asks questions that require more thought.
6. Tells students whether their answers are right or wrong.
7. Gives specific praise.
8. Gives reasons for praise.
9. Listens.
10. Accepts feelings of the student.
11. Gets within an arm's reach of each student each day.
12. Is courteous to students.
13. Shows personal interest and gives compliments.
14. Touches students (appropriately).
15. Desists (he or she does not call attention to every negative behavior).

Note. From TESA (Teacher Expectations & Student Achievement), Los Angeles Department of Education.

Creating an Environment of Mutual Respect

- Know something about each student.
- Engage in behaviors that indicate affection for each student.
- Bring student interests into content and personalize learning activities.
- Engage in physical behaviors that communicate interest in students.
- Use humor when appropriate.
- Consistently enforce positive and negative consequences.

–Robert J. Marzano, *The Art and Science of Teaching,* 2007

10 Actions to Educate Students

10 Actions to Educate Students

2. Hidden Rules

Teach students the hidden rules of school.

Why?

Hidden rules break relationships, and without relationships learning is decreased.

Could You Survive in Poverty?

Put a check by each item you know how to do.

____ 1. I know which churches and sections of town have the best rummage sales.

____ 2. I know when Walmart, drug stores, and convenience stores throw away over-the-counter medicine with expired dates.

____ 3. I know which pawn shops sell DVDs for $1.

____ 4. In my town in criminal courts, I know which judges are lenient, which ones are crooked, and which ones are fair.

____ 5. I know how to physically fight and defend myself physically.

____ 6. I know how to get a gun, even if I have a police record.

____ 7. I know how to keep my clothes from being stolen at the Laundromat.

____ 8. I know what problems to look for in a used car.

____ 9. I/my family use a payday lender.

____ 10. I know how to live without electricity and a phone.

____ 11. I know how to use a knife as scissors.

____ 12. I can entertain a group of friends with my personality and my stories.

____ 13. I know which churches will provide assistance with food or shelter.

____ 14. I know how to move in half a day.

____ 15. I know how to get and use food stamps or an electronic card for benefits.

____ 16. I know where the free medical clinics are.

____ 17. I am very good at trading and bartering.

____ 18. I can get by without a car.

____ 19. I know how to hide my car so the repo man cannot find it.

____ 20. We pay our cable-TV bill before we pay our rent.

____ 21. I know which sections of town "belong" to which gangs.

10 Actions to Educate Students

Could You Survive in Middle Class?

Put a check by each item you know how to do.

_____ 1. I know how to get my children into Little League, piano lessons, soccer, etc.

_____ 2. I have an online checking account and monitor my bills online.

_____ 3. Every bedroom has its own TV and DVD player.

_____ 4. My children know the best name brands in clothing.

_____ 5. I know how to order in a nice restaurant.

_____ 6. I know how to use a credit card, checking account, and savings account—and I understand an annuity. I understand term life insurance, disability insurance, and 20/80 medical insurance policy, as well as house insurance, flood insurance, and replacement insurance.

_____ 7. I talk to my children about going to college.

_____ 8. I know how to get one of the best interest rates on my new-car loan.

_____ 9. I understand the difference among the principal, interest, and escrow statements on my house payment.

_____ 10. I know how to help my children with their homework and do not hesitate to call the school if I need additional information.

_____ 11. I know how to decorate the house for the different holidays.

_____ 12. I/my family belong to an athletic or exercise club.

_____ 13. I know how to use most of the tools in the garage.

_____ 14. I repair items in my house almost immediately when they break—or know a repair service and call it.

_____ 15. We have more than one computer in our home.

_____ 16. We plan our vacations six months to a year in advance.

_____ 17. I contribute to a retirement plan separate from Social Security.

Could You Survive in Wealth?

Put a check by each item you know how to do.

_____ 1. I can read a menu in at least three languages.

_____ 2. I have several favorite restaurants in different countries of the world. I use a *concierge* to book the best restaurants as I travel throughout the world.

_____ 3. During the holidays, I know how to hire a decorator to identify the appropriate themes and items with which to decorate the house.

_____ 4. I know who my preferred financial adviser, legal firm, certified public accounting firm, designer, florist, caterer, domestic employment service, and hairdresser are. In addition, I have a preferred tailor, travel agency, and personal trainer.

_____ 5. I have at least two residences that are staffed and maintained.

_____ 6. I know how to ensure confidentiality and loyalty from my domestic staff.

_____ 7. I have at least two or three "screens" that keep people whom I do not wish to see away from me.

_____ 8. I fly in my own plane, the company plane, or first class.

_____ 9. I know how to enroll my children in the preferred private schools.

_____ 10. I know how to host the parties that "key" people attend.

_____ 11. I am on the boards of at least two charities.

_____ 12. I contribute to at least four or five political campaigns.

_____ 13. I support or buy the work of a particular artist.

_____ 14. I know how to read a corporate financial statement and analyze my own financial statements.

_____ 15. I belong to at least one private club (country club, yacht club, etc.).

_____ 16. I own more vehicles than there are drivers.

_____ 17. I "buy a table" at several charity events throughout the year.

_____ 18. I have worldwide coverage on my cell phone for both text and voice messages, as well as e-mail.

_____ 19. I have the provenance for all original art, jewelry, antiques, and one-of-a-kind items.

_____ 20. I easily translate exchange rates for currency between and among different countries.

Could you cope with a spouse/partner who came from old money (or had that mindset)?

It would bother me if my spouse or partner:

☐ Spent money on private club memberships.

☐ Had a trust fund from birth.

☐ Insisted on the artistic quality and merit of household items, clothing, accessories, and so on.

☐ Had a personal assistant to assist with purchases of clothing and accessories.

☐ Spent money on a personal tailor and physical trainer.

☐ Spent a great deal of time on charitable activities and did not make or take money for that time.

☐ Placed our children in the care of a nanny.

☐ Insisted that our children be placed in private boarding schools at the age of six.

☐ Talked a lot about the presentation of food.

☐ Staffed and maintained homes in more than one country.

☐ Spent money on a private airplane and/or yacht.

☐ Established trust funds for our children at birth.

☐ Maintained social and financial connections with individuals whom I didn't like.

☐ Had family members who looked down on me because of my bloodline or pedigree (or lack thereof).

☐ Kept an accountant, lawyer, domestic service agency, and investment broker on retainer.

☐ Was adamant about details, insisting on perfection in virtually everything.

☐ Wanted to have nothing further to do with a decent individual who didn't have a suitable connection.

☐ Spent $1 million-plus on an original piece of art, and would *only* purchase original works of art.

☐ Attended an Ivy League college or university.

☐ Valued me largely for my social connections.

☐ Reviewed family assets and liabilities on a monthly basis.

☐ Purchased furniture and furnishings for their artistic merit or designer designation.

☐ Kept almost no food in the house.

Note. From *Crossing the Tracks for Love,* by Ruby K. Payne, 2005.

Could you cope with a spouse/partner who came from middle class (or had that mindset)?

It would bother me if my spouse or partner:

- ☐ Spent long hours at the office.
- ☐ Required our household to run on a budget.
- ☐ Planned out our week in advance.
- ☐ Started a college fund at the birth of our child.
- ☐ Hired a plumber to do a needed repair.
- ☐ Fixed the plumbing himself/herself.
- ☐ Played golf every weekend with his buddies.
- ☐ Kept a job that he/she hates for financial reasons.
- ☐ Rigidly adhered to time demands—and was often early.
- ☐ Was organized, keeping a paper trail on everything.
- ☐ Refused to give money to relatives who weren't working.
- ☐ Refused to allow a relative to come live with us.
- ☐ Planned vacations a year in advance.
- ☐ Spent evenings taking graduate courses.
- ☐ Devoted considerable time to a community charitable event.
- ☐ Shopped for high-quality clothing/shoes/accessories, then charged those items.
- ☐ Withdrew TV, computer, and other privileges from the children as part of discipline.
- ☐ Paid for our child's college expenses and tuition.
- ☐ Paid for tennis, golf, dance, swimming, and other types of lessons for our child.
- ☐ Often made a big issue over the quality of food.
- ☐ Bought reprints and numbered artwork as part of our home's décor.
- ☐ Purchased furniture for its practicality and match to the décor.
- ☐ Had family members who discounted me because of my lack of education or achievement.

10 Actions to Educate Students

Note. From *Crossing the Tracks for Love,* by Ruby K. Payne, 2005.

Could you cope with a spouse/partner who came from generational poverty (or had that mindset)?

It would bother me if my spouse or partner:

☐ Repeatedly gave money to a relative who would not work.

☐ Left household bills unpaid in order to give money to a relative.

☐ Loaned the car to a relative who doesn't have insurance and cannot be insured.

☐ Allowed a relative to move in and stay with you.

☐ Didn't pay attention to time (e.g., missed dates, was extremely late, didn't show).

☐ Quit jobs without having another one because he/she didn't like the boss.

☐ Cursed at his/her boss in public.

☐ Physically fought—fairly frequently.

☐ Didn't think education was important.

☐ Left items in the house unrepaired.

☐ Used physical punishment on the children as part of discipline.

☐ Viewed himself as a "fighter" or a "lover" who works hard physically.

☐ Served food from the stove, and ate most meals in front of the TV.

☐ Almost always had the TV and/or radio on, and often loudly.

☐ Kept the house dark on the inside—poorly lit and with window coverings closed.

☐ Kept organizational patterns of household chaotic.

☐ Bought clothing from secondhand stores, garage sales, and so on.

☐ Bought designer clothing or shoes for our children, but didn't pay an urgent household bill.

☐ Made a big deal about the quantity of food.

☐ Viewed me as a possession.

☐ Had family members who made fun of me for having a college degree.

☐ Bragged about me by talking badly about me.

☐ Chose to spend time with relatives, rather than spending time with me.

☐ Purchased alcoholic beverages for entertainment before paying for necessities (e.g., car insurance, utilities, rent).

Note. From *Crossing the Tracks for Love,* by Ruby K. Payne, 2005.

Hidden Rules of Economic Class

	POVERTY	MIDDLE CLASS	WEALTH
POSSESSIONS	People.	Things.	One-of-a-kind objects, legacies, pedigrees.
MONEY	To be used, spent.	To be managed.	To be conserved, invested.
PERSONALITY	Is for entertainment. Sense of humor is highly valued.	Is for acquisition and stability. Achievement is highly valued.	Is for connections. Financial, political, social connections are highly valued.
SOCIAL EMPHASIS	Social inclusion of people they like.	Emphasis is on self-governance and self-sufficiency.	Emphasis is on social exclusion.
FOOD	Key question: Did you have enough? Quantity important.	Key question: Did you like it? Quality important.	Key question: Was it presented well? Presentation important.
CLOTHING	Clothing valued for individual style and expression of personality.	Clothing valued for its quality and acceptance into norms of middle class. Label important.	Clothing valued for its artistic sense and expression. Designer important.
TIME	Present most important. Decisions made for moment based on feelings or survival.	Future most important. Decisions made against future ramifications.	Traditions and past history most important. Decisions made partially on basis of tradition decorum.
EDUCATION	Valued and revered as abstract but not as reality. Education is about facts.	Crucial for climbing success ladder and making money.	Necessary tradition for making and maintaining connections.
DESTINY	Believes in fate. Cannot do much to mitigate chance.	Believes in choice. Can change future with good choices now.	*Noblesse oblige.*
LANGUAGE	Casual register. Language is about survival.	Formal register. Language is about negotiation.	Formal register. Language is about connections.
FAMILY STRUCTURE	Tends to be matriarchal.	Tends to be patriarchal.	Depends on who has/ controls money.
WORLD VIEW	Sees world in terms of local setting.	Sees world in terms of national setting.	Sees world in terms of international view.
LOVE	Love and acceptance conditional, based on whether individual is liked.	Love and acceptance conditional, based largely on achievement.	Love and acceptance conditional, related to social standing and connections.
DRIVING FORCES	Survival, relationships, entertainment.	Work and achievement.	Financial, political, social connections.
HUMOR	About people and sex.	About situations.	About social *faux pas.*

Key Points

Hidden rules about time and money:

Poverty	Middle Class	Wealth
Survival	Work	Political connections
Relationships	Achievement	Financial connections
Entertainment	Material security	Social connections

We can neither excuse nor scold our students. We must teach them.

We must teach students that there are two sets of rules.

Example: Basketball does not have the same rules as football.

Penance/Forgiveness Cycle

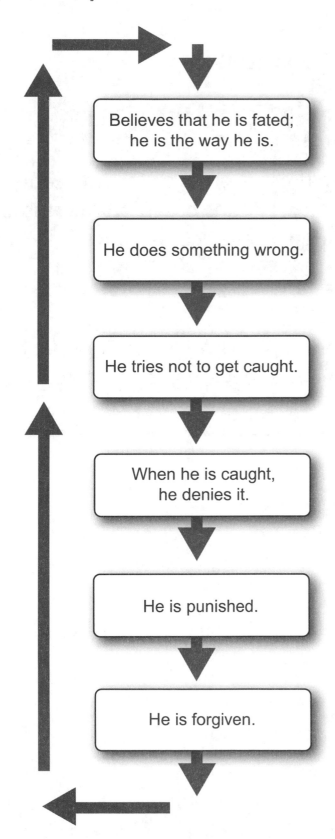

Believes that he is fated;
he is the way he is.

He does something wrong.

He tries not to get caught.

When he is caught,
he denies it.

He is punished.

He is forgiven.

10 Actions to Educate Students

3. Resources

Analyze the resources of your students, and make interventions based on the resources the students have access to.

Why?

Interventions do not work if they are based on resources that are not available.

Resources

FINANCIAL
Having the money to purchase goods and services.

EMOTIONAL
Being able to choose and control emotional responses, particularly to negative situations, without engaging in self-destructive behavior. This is an internal resource and shows itself through stamina, perseverance, and choices.

MENTAL
Having the mental abilities and acquired skills (reading, writing, computing) to deal with daily life.

SPIRITUAL
Believing in divine purpose and guidance.

PHYSICAL
Having physical health and mobility.

SUPPORT SYSTEMS
Having friends, family, and backup resources available to access in times of need. These are external resources.

RELATIONSHIPS/ROLE MODELS
Having frequent access to adult(s) who are appropriate, who are nurturing to the child, and who do not engage in self-destructive behavior.

KNOWLEDGE OF HIDDEN RULES
Knowing the unspoken cues and habits of a group.

FORMAL REGISTER
Having the vocabulary, language ability, and negotiation skills necessary to succeed in school and/or work settings.

Resource Analysis

Name	Financial resources	Emotional resources	Mental resources	Spiritual resources	Physical resources	Support systems	Relationships/role models	Knowledge of hidden rules	Formal register

Resource Scenario
Young female student in rural elementary school

Background

Rosalinda lives in a rural area of the United States. There are 400 students, K–12, in her school. Rosalinda is in second grade and lives with her grandparents most of the time. Her grandparents fought through the courts to get full custody but were unable to get it. Her mother is in prison, and her father is an alcoholic but a good friend of the local police chief; her dad is employed by the chief's prominent, land-owning family. So when her father gets drunk, someone simply takes him home. One of the reasons the grandparents filed to have custody is because he often takes Rosalinda with him when he drinks.

Due to the amount of drugs her mother took during pregnancy, Rosalinda is severely dyslexic but has a sweet personality and is determined to do well in school. Her grandmother tutors her every day; her grandparents take her to church twice a week. Sometimes Rosalinda will call her grandmother and tell her to come get her because her father is drunk. Together, her grandparents make more than $100,000 a year. Rosalinda's learning disability makes schooling difficult for her; math is especially problematic. Furthermore, after her father has had one of his drinking bouts, it's hard for her to concentrate. It's also hard for her to have friends because the other parents won't let their children go to her house because of her dad.

What are Rosalinda's resources? What interventions might make a difference for Rosalinda?

Using a scale of 0 to 4 (4 being high), how would you assess Rosalinda's resource base? Put a question mark if you are uncertain or if that information is not available or cannot be inferred.

RESOURCE	Rosalinda (student)
Financial	
Emotional	
Mental	
Spiritual	
Physical	
Support systems	
Relationships/role models	
Knowledge of hidden rules of school and work	
Formal register	

10 Actions to Educate Students

Resource Scenario
Second-language immigrant student

Background

Siaka has been in the United States for two years. She is 14 years old. There was so much war in her native country that she was lucky to get out alive. She saw two of her brothers get killed. Her mother and father have come to the United States as well. Her father has a college degree in his native country, and her mother had 10 years of schooling in their country. Because of the war's disruption, Siaka had only five years of formal schooling.

Siaka has been placed in seventh grade in your classroom. She is rapidly learning English but is very quiet. She often doesn't do homework, and when you ask her about her homework, she won't reply. She's in danger of failing your class because she doesn't do enough of the work. She has one friend, Nasha, also from her native country, who is very social but not academically motivated. Nasha tells you that Siaka has bad dreams and cannot get her homework done. Nasha tells you that she and Siaka will soon be marrying young men from their culture. You called the mother about Siaka's school situation, but the mother did not understand your English. Siaka has three younger siblings, and her mother works two jobs at minimum wage. The father drives a cab, and he is learning English.

Siaka gets free lunches but rarely eats the food. She keeps her eyes down most of the time. She is a beautiful young lady, and the boys try to talk to her, but she is shy. In physical education, she will not dress out, and her parents have gotten an exception for her by bringing a note from a doctor.

What are Siaka's resources? What interventions might you make to help Siaka be successful?

Using a scale of 0 to 4 (4 being high), how would you assess Siaka's resource base? Put a question mark if you are uncertain or if that information is not available or cannot be inferred.

RESOURCE	Siaka (student)
Financial	
Emotional	
Mental	
Spiritual	
Physical	
Support systems	
Relationships/role models	
Knowledge of hidden rules of school and work	
Formal register	

Resource Scenario
Middle school boy from a mid-size town

Background

Duane is a 12-year-old African-American boy who lives with his father and two younger siblings in public housing. His mother left when Duane was 6, leaving his father with three children under the age of 7. Duane goes directly home after school each day to watch his younger siblings while his father is at work. There is often nothing but baloney and Kool-Aid for dinner. Duane is responsible for feeding his siblings, bathing them, helping with homework, and getting them to bed. This leaves Duane little time for his own homework. School is a struggle for Duane, but he is a gifted athlete. He has already drawn the interest of the high school football coach who believes he has a bright future as a player.

You are Duane's father, Roney, a 29-year-old male. Duane was born while you were a junior in high school and his mother, Cydney, was 16. You and Cydney were married shortly after Duane was born. You dropped out of school to work to support Duane and his mother. You had a good job changing oil at a local service station and were able to support your wife and child so Cydney could stay home. Duane's brother, Walker, was born four years later, but Cydney had a difficult pregnancy, and soon after the station you worked at closed. Cydney became despondent and often went out with friends, leaving you with the children. You were able to take odd jobs fixing cars but didn't make enough to support your family. You and the children were forced to move in with your mother, who was in her mid-50s and an alcoholic. She was on disability with a fixed income and struggled herself to make ends meet. With your mother there to watch the children at night while Cydney went out, you were able to secure a minimum-wage position as a delivery driver. Between the odd jobs fixing cars during the day and the delivery job at night, you were beginning to catch up financially. After your third child was born, Cydney left you without warning and moved to a distant state. Within a month, your mother lost her battle with alcoholism and died.

Current situation

You leave for work before your children get home from school. You are dependent on Duane to help with your other children at night so you can work. However, Duane is becoming more frustrated with school and is causing problems. His teacher calls to set up a parent-teacher conference, which means you will be late for work. You want Duane to graduate because you know the importance of an education, so you make it a priority to get involved. At the meeting, the high school coach is present and expresses his interest in Duane's ability. He says playing football would help Duane build self-esteem and work harder to succeed in school. The teacher agrees and thinks Duane should practice with the high school team after school two days a week. He also offers to stay after school to tutor Duane and help him with his reading comprehension.

You want Duane to have the opportunity to play football because you feel it will help him build self-confidence, which in turn will help him in school. You also appreciate the teacher offering help academically and you understand Duane needs extra help. But you need Duane at home to watch his siblings so you can work. There is no one else to watch your two youngest children.

Using a scale of 0 to 4 (4 being high), how would you assess the resource base of Duane and Roney? Put a question mark if you are uncertain or if that information is not available or cannot be inferred.

RESOURCE	Duane (student)	Roney (father)
Financial		
Emotional		
Mental		
Spiritual		
Physical		
Support systems		
Relationships/role models		
Knowledge of hidden rules of school and work		
Formal register		

Resource Scenario
Male student in rural high school

Background

Wadell is a 17-year-old Native American male. His father was killed two years ago in an auto accident. His mother is serving the first year of a three-year prison sentence for felony possession of methamphetamine. Wadell and his 11-year-old sister, Destinie, live with their grandmother who lives in a one-bedroom trailer in a small community on the reservation. The trailer is old, does not have running water or electricity, and the family is often without fuel to run the generator and without food to eat. Grandmother cares for the children, but due to age is not always able to provide support. Wadell hasn't learned to drive, and public transportation is not available, so he and Destinie walk everywhere. When he isn't at school, Wadell spends most of his time caring for Destinie and his grandmother. Sometimes their "cousin brother," who lives 300 miles away, comes to visit, but he doesn't stay very long. Wadell and Destinie both qualify for and receive tribal services (e.g., clothing and medical services). Wadell values tradition, attends tribal gatherings and pow-wows and wants to learn more about his family and culture. He especially loves the drums and songs.

You first met Wadell when he was a student in your ninth-grade class. He confides in you and another teacher at the high school. After the death of his father, Wadell swore he would never drink or do drugs. For the past three years Wadell has scored at the advanced level in mathematics on the state math assessment.

Current situation

Wadell and Destinie have nearly perfect attendance. Since Wadell transferred to the alternative high school, his grades have improved, and his current GPA is 3.0. His technology skills are exceptional; he loves all types of music, works as an assistant in the school's technology lab, and creates sound tracks and digital art. Wadell tends to be very quiet and doesn't talk much, but he has shared his dream of taking Destinie and his mother to Disney World, owning a music company, and having his own record label.

Students admire Wadell's talent and strength, but he has doesn't have a best friend, nor does he associate with one specific group of students. You and Wadell have a relationship of mutual respect and meet at school regularly to discuss his progress and options. After reviewing this year's final grades and his transcript, you realize that Wadell can graduate at mid-term next school year.

What resources does Wadell have? What additional resources and options are available? How would you go about assisting Wadell in accessing them? What resources are available to Destinie? Choose one student to assess.

Using a scale of 0 to 4 (4 being high), how would you assess the resource base of Wadell or Destinie and their grandmother? Put a question mark if you are uncertain or if that information is not available or cannot be inferred.

RESOURCE	Wadell or Destinie (students)	Grandmother
Financial		
Emotional		
Mental		
Spiritual		
Physical		
Support systems		
Relationships/role models		
Knowledge of hidden rules of school and work		
Formal register		

Resource Scenario
Male student in inner-city high school

Background

Raymond is a Hispanic male, and his father is a skilled-labor employee. Since before Raymond could walk, his father referred to him as his little football hero. Raymond's father was considered to be passionate and aggressive. Up until eighth grade, Raymond often witnessed his father make degrading remarks to his mother. Raymond was encouraged to play and perfect his football techniques, and his grades followed a predictable pattern during most of his academic career. He would fail throughout most of the grading period. As the time for report cards approached, his father would make a call or an appointment with his teacher(s) and request that Raymond be allowed to make up some of his grades or be given an opportunity for extra credit. While not always successful, it worked often enough for Raymond to get promoted year after year.

One month after Raymond's 13th birthday, his mother told him of her intentions to divorce his father. That day his mother noticed Raymond speaking to her in the same harsh manner her husband had been for many years. Raymond blamed his mother for all of the family troubles. Between eighth and 11th grade, Raymond lived between two households. His parents got along better as a result of the divorce, and relations were amicable for the most part.

When Raymond qualified for the football team, his father expressed great pride to anyone who would listen. He attended every football game; Raymond's mother came to most of them and sat with her friends. Despite Raymond's success on the football field, his relations with authority figures (particularly females) grew increasingly defiant. His father's interventions on his son's behalf became less and less successful during Raymond's high school years, and he soon started blaming Raymond's teachers for his son's academic struggles.

Current situation

Raymond has made a name for himself on the football field. He has obvious talent that has been noticed by some college scouts. When his academic records are looked at, he is told that there are concerns but that he can be provided tutors if certain conditions are met. As a result of this and some earnest conversation with school staff members who have expressed concern about Raymond, he begins to examine his decision-making process. He comes to realize that he has never taken school seriously and how academics will play an important role in college—and in his vocational pursuits.

Following some painful self-examination, Raymond announces that he is quitting football in order to concentrate more on his grades. Staff members are stunned by his decision. Raymond begins to take ownership of his temper and becomes more studious, however difficult. Some of his teachers begin to notice that increasingly they are talking to his mother, while his father has become less accessible. It is mid-year before his teachers learn that Raymond's father cut his son off in every way after learning of his decision to quit football. Raymond now faces the reality that he is too far behind in his classes to catch up and graduate with his friends—and can no longer depend on his father for support. In late November, Raymond drops out of school.

Using a scale of 0 to 4 (4 being high), how would you assess the resource base of Raymond and his mother and father? Put a question mark if you are uncertain or if that information is not available or cannot be inferred.

RESOURCE	Raymond (student)	Mother and father
Financial		
Emotional		
Mental		
Spiritual		
Physical		
Support systems		
Relationships/role models		
Knowledge of hidden rules of school and work		
Formal register		

Resource Scenario
Elementary school boy from mid-size town

Background

John is an 8-year-old Caucasian boy. His father is a doctor and remarried but does not see his children. He pays minimal child support. The mother, Adele, works part time and is an alcoholic. One younger sibling, a girl who is mentally and physically handicapped, lives with the mother and John.

You are Adele, John's mother. You are a 29-year-old female. You quit college your sophomore year so that you could go to work to support John's father as he went through medical school. You were both elated when John was born. During the time your husband was an intern, you found that a drink or two or three in the evening calmed you down, especially since your husband was gone so much. When your second child was born, she was severely handicapped. Both of you were in shock. A year later your husband finished his residency, announced that he was in love with another woman—and divorced you. Last you heard, your husband is driving a Porsche, and he and his new wife spent their most recent vacation in Cancún. Your parents are deceased. You have a sister who lives 50 miles away. Your weekly income, including child support, is $300 before taxes. Your handicapped child is 3 years old and is in daycare provided by the school district.

Current situation

You have been late to work for the third time this month. Your car broke down, and it will take $400 to fix it. Your boss told you that you will be docked for a day's pay—and that if you're late again, you will be fired. You don't know how you're going to get to work tomorrow. You consider several options: (1) You can go car shopping, (2) you can put the car in the garage and worry about the money later, (3) you can invite the mechanic over for dinner, (4) you can get mad and quit your job, (5) you can call your ex and threaten to take him back to court unless he pays for the car, (6) you can try to get a second job, or (7) you can get drunk.

Your daughter has had another seizure, and you took her to the doctor (one of the reasons you were late for work). The new medicine will cost you $45 every month.

John comes home from school and announces that the school is going to have a reading contest. Every book you read with him will earn points for him. Each book is one point, and he wants to earn 100 points. You must do physical therapy with your daughter each evening for 30 minutes, as well as get dinner. For John to get his books, he needs you to go to the library with him. You have only enough gas to go to work and back for the rest of the week, maybe not that. He also tells you that the school is having an open house, and he will get a pencil if you come. But John is not old enough to watch your daughter. Your ex has already threatened to bring up in court that you are an unfit mother if you try to get more money from him.

The mechanic calls and invites you out to dinner. He tells you that the two of you might be able to work something out in terms of payment. It has been a long time since you have been out, and he is good-looking and seems like a nice man.

What are Adele's and John's resources?

Using a scale of 0 to 4 (4 being high), how would you assess the resource base of Adele and John? Put a question mark if you are uncertain or if that information is not available or cannot be inferred.

RESOURCE	Adele (mother)	John (student)
Financial		
Emotional		
Mental		
Spiritual		
Physical		
Support systems		
Relationships/role models		
Knowledge of hidden rules of school and work		
Formal register		

Creating Interventions

RESOURCE	QUESTIONS TO DETERMINE BEST INTERVENTION
Financial	<ul><li>Can the student afford the field trip, or is a scholarship needed for him/her?</li><li>Can the student afford supplies for the project/science fair/other activity?</li><li>Is the student hungry, or must a linkage to food be found?</li></ul>
Emotional	<ul><li>Can the student verbalize choices?</li><li>Does the student have the language to mediate situations without resorting to fists?</li></ul>
Mental	<ul><li>Can the student read at his/her grade level?</li><li>Can the student identify the final product or task?</li><li>Does the student know what will be evaluated and how?</li></ul>
Spiritual	<ul><li>Does the student believe he/she has some control over the situation, or does he/she say there is nothing he/she can do?</li><li>Does the student have a future story and a plan to go with it?</li></ul>
Physical	<ul><li>Is the student clean?</li><li>Are the student's clothes clean?</li><li>Can the student physically take care of himself/herself?</li></ul>
Support systems	<ul><li>Is the student the primary support system for his/her household?</li><li>Is there enough stability in the home that the student can have a place to keep and do work?</li></ul>
Relationships/ role models	<ul><li>Does the student have at least one adult who is nurturing and caring?</li><li>Does the student have three or more adults who care about him/her?</li><li>Are all of his/her significant relationships with peers?</li></ul>
Knowledge of hidden rules	<ul><li>Does the student use the "appropriate" school response to situations?</li><li>Does the student try to be invisible?</li></ul>
Formal register	<ul><li>Does the student have access to formal register at home?</li><li>Does the student get right to the point when telling a story? Does the student begin at the end of the story and tell the story in no particular order?</li></ul>

10 Actions to Educate Students

10 Actions to Educate Students

4. Formal Register

Teach formal register, the language of school and work.

Why?

To understand written text, which is essential for success at school and work.

Registers of Language

REGISTER	EXPLANATION
FROZEN	Language that is always the same. For example: Lord's Prayer, wedding vows, etc.
FORMAL	The standard sentence syntax and word choice of work and school. Has complete sentences and specific word choice.
CONSULTATIVE	Formal register when used in conversation. Discourse pattern not quite as direct as formal register.
CASUAL	Language between friends characterized by a 400- to 800-word vocabulary. Word choice general and not specific. Conversation dependent upon non-verbal assists. Sentence syntax often incomplete.
INTIMATE	Language between lovers or twins. Language of sexual harassment.

Note. Adapted from Martin Joos, 1967.

Research About Language in Children, Ages 1 to 4, in Stable Households by Economic Group			
Number of words exposed to	**Economic group**	**Affirmations (strokes)**	**Prohibitions (discounts)**
13 million words	Welfare	1 for every	2
26 million words	Working class	2 for every	1
45 million words	Professional	6 for every	1

Note. From *Meaningful Differences in the Everyday Experience of Young American Children,* by B. Hart and T. R. Risley, 1995.

Story Structure

Formal

Plot

B   E

Casual

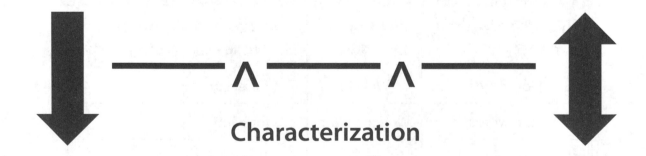

Characterization

10 Actions to Educate Students

5. Abstract processes

Teach abstract processes.

Why?

All learning involves *what, why,* and *how.* The *how* piece must be direct-taught for tasks to be done.

Mediation

Mental Prowess

MEDIATION		
Identification of the stimulus	**Assignment of meaning**	**Identification of a strategy**

What
Don't cross the street without looking.

Why
You might get run over by a car.

How
Look both ways twice before crossing the street.

Cognitive Strategies

INPUT:
Quantity and quality of
data gathered

1. Use planning behaviors.
2. Focus perception on specific stimulus.
3. Control impulsivity.
4. Explore data systematically.
5. Use appropriate and accurate labels.
6. Organize space using stable systems of reference.
7. Orient data in time.
8. Identify constancies across variations.
9. Gather precise and accurate data.
10. Consider two sources of information at once.
11. Organize data (parts of a whole).
12. Visually transport data.

ELABORATION:
Efficient use of data

1. Identify and define the problem.
2. Select relevant cues.
3. Compare data.
4. Select appropriate categories of time.
5. Summarize data.
6. Project relationships of data.
7. Use logical data.
8. Test hypothesis.
9. Build inferences.
10. Make a plan using the data.
11. Use appropriate labels.
12. Use data systematically.

OUTPUT:
Communication of elaboration
and input

1. Communicate clearly the labels and processes.
2. Visually transport data correctly.
3. Use precise and accurate language.
4. Control impulsive behavior.

10 Actions to Educate Students

Note. Adapted from work of Reuven Feuerstein

What Does This Mean in the Classroom?

When a student cannot:	One will often see this:
Use planning behaviors ...	Does not get his/her work done; is impulsive.
Focus perception on a specific stimulus ...	Misses parts of the task; cannot find the information on the page.
Control impulsivity ...	Cannot plan.
Explore data systematically ...	Does not have a method for checking work, for getting all the work done, and for finding complete answers.
Use appropriate and accurate labels (vocabulary) ...	Does not have the words to explain; cannot label processes; uses generic words, e.g., "Get that thing."
Organize space with stable systems of reference ...	Cannot read a map; cannot use the procedures in math.
Orient data in time ...	Cannot sequence or plan; cannot follow directions.
Identify constancies across variations ...	Cannot make judgments or generalizations; cannot identify patterns.
Gather precise and accurate data ...	Cannot tell specifically when, where, and how something happened.
Consider two sources of information at once ...	Cannot compare and contrast; does a different assignment the way the first one was done, whether appropriate or not.
Organize data (parts of a whole) ...	Cannot explain why; does not recognize when something is missing.
Visually transport data ...	Cannot cheat because he/she cannot copy.

10 Actions to Educate Students

6. Mental models

Provide mental models.

Why?

Mental models translate between the abstract representational world and the sensory concrete world.

The Paper World of Middle Class

To survive in school or at work, you have to be verbal, abstract, and proactive. You have to plan.

School and work are an abstract representational world. For each of the items listed, what does the paper represent in the sensory world? Two examples are given.

ABSTRACT ITEM	REPRESENTS
Grades	The ticket to get into college, a better job, more money
House deed	The physical property
Address	
Social Security number	
Daily to-do list	
Clock or calendar	
State assessment	
Homework	
Insurance papers	
Driver's license	
TV guide	
Photograph	
Letters in the alphabet	
Numbers	
Musical notations	
Road map	
Sonogram	
MRI	
Trust document	
Student handbook	
Teacher contract	
Menu	

A mental model is a story, analogy, or a drawing.

Mental models translate between the sensory and the abstract.

10 Actions to Educate Students

7. Planning

Teach students how to plan.

Why?

To control impulsivity for task completion.

If an individual depends upon a random, episodic story structure for memory patterns, lives in an unpredictable environment, *and has not developed the ability to plan,* then …

If an individual cannot plan, he or she *cannot predict.*

If an individual cannot predict, he or she *cannot identify cause and effect.*

If an individual cannot identify cause and effect, he or she *cannot identify consequence.*

If an individual cannot identify consequence, he or she *cannot control impulsivity.*

If an individual cannot control impulsivity, he or she

_____.

Planning Backwards

Step 1: State the desired end, goal, or future picture.
Step 2: List the end date or product in the last column on the right.
Step 3: In each section or column list what actions or steps will be
taken to accomplish or reach the goal or outcome.
Step 4: Monitor progress and adjust as needed.

A tool to start with the outcome or future picture, break it into parts, and develop action steps.

State the goal or outcome:						
Date	Date	Date	Date	Date	Date	Date

10 Actions to Educate Students

8. Voices

Use the adult voice and reframing to change behaviors.

Why?

To maintain relationships and get the appropriate behaviors.

Voices

Child
- Quit picking on me.
- You don't love me.
- You want me to leave.
- Nobody likes (loves) me.
- I hate you.
- You're ugly.
- You make me sick.
- It's your fault.
- Don't blame me.
- She, he, _____ did it.
- You make me mad.

Parent
- You shouldn't (should) do that.
- It's wrong (right) to do _____.
- That's stupid, immature, out of line, ridiculous.
- Life's not fair. Get busy.
- You are good, bad, worthless, beautiful (any judgmental, evaluative comment).
- You do as I say.
- If you weren't so _____, this wouldn't happen to you.
- Why can't you be like _____?

Adult
- In what ways could this be resolved?
- What factors will be used to determine the effectiveness, quality of …?
- I would like to recommend _____.
- What are choices in this situation?
- I am comfortable (uncomfortable) with _____.
- Options that could be considered are _____.
- For me to be comfortable, I need the following things to occur: _____.
- These are the consequences of that choice/action: _____.
- We agree to disagree.

Note. Adapted from work of Eric Berne, 1996.

Ruby K. Payne, Ph.D.

Poverty Series   Part III

Working With Students From Poverty: Discipline

By Ruby K. Payne, Ph.D.
Founder of aha! Process, Inc.

In poverty, discipline is often about penance and forgiveness. Because love is unconditional and because the time frame is the present, the notion that discipline should be instructive and change behavior is not a part of the culture in generational poverty. In matriarchal, generational poverty, the mother is the most powerful position and is in some ways "keeper of the soul," so she dispenses the judgments, determines the amount and price of penance, and gives forgiveness. When forgiveness is granted, behaviors and activities return to the way they were before the incident.

It is important to note that the approach is to teach a separate set of behaviors. Many of the behaviors students bring to school help them survive outside of school. Students learn and use many different rules depending on the video game they are playing. Likewise, they need to learn to use different rules to be successful in the setting they are in. If poor students do not know how to fight physically, they are going to be in danger on the streets. But if that is their only method for resolving a problem, then they cannot be successful in school.

The culture of poverty does not provide for success in the middle class, because the middle class to a large extent requires the self-governance of behavior. To be successful in work and in school requires the self-governance of behavior. What then do schools need to do to teach appropriate behavior?

Structure and Choice

The two anchors of any effective discipline program that moves students to self-governance are structure and choice. The program must clearly outline the expected behaviors and the consequences of not choosing those behaviors. The program must also emphasize that the individual always has choice – to follow or not to follow the expected behaviors. With each choice then comes consequence – either desirable or not desirable. Many discipline workshops use this approach and are available to schools.

When the focus is, "I'll tell you what to do and when," the student can never move from dependence to independence. He or she is always at the level of dependence.

Behavior Analysis

Mentally or in writing, teachers or administrators must first examine the behavior analysis:

1. Decide what behaviors the child needs to have to be successful.
2. Does the child have the resources to develop those behaviors?
3. Will it help to contact a parent?

Are resources available through them? What resources are available through the school district?

4. How will behaviors be taught?
5. What are other choices the child could make?
6. What will help the child repeat the successful behavior?

When these questions are completed, they provide answers to the strategies that will most help the student. The chart on the next page indicates possible explanations of behaviors and possible interventions.

Participation of the Student

While the teacher or administrator is analyzing, the student must analyze as well. To help students do so, give them this four-part questionnaire. This has been used with students as young as second semester, first grade. Students have the most difficulty with question number three. Basically, they see no other choices available than the one they have made.

> **Name:**
> 1. **What did you do?**
> 2. **When you did that, what did you want?**
> 3. **List four other things you could have done.**
> 4. **What will you do next time?**

In going over the sheet with the student, it is important to discuss other choices that could have been made. Students often do not have

> **The culture of poverty does not provide for success in the middle class, because the middle class to a large extent requires the self-governance of behavior.**

page 1

10 Actions to Educate Students

Ruby K. Payne, Ph.D.   Poverty Series   Part III

10 Actions to Educate Students

Behavior Related to Poverty	Intervention
Laughs when disciplined. A way to save face in matriarchal poverty.	*Understand the reason for the behavior. Tell the student three or four other behaviors that would be more appropriate.*
Argues loudly with the teacher. Poverty is participatory, and the culture has a distrust of authority. Sees the system as inherently dishonest and unfair.	*Don't argue with the student. Have them complete the four-part questionnaire on page 1. Model respect for students.*
Angry response. Anger is based on fear. The question is what the fear is – loss of face?	*Respond in the adult voice. When the student cools down, discuss other responses that could be used.*
Inappropriate or vulgar comments. They rely on casual register, may not know formal register.	*Make students generate or teach students other phrases that could be used to say the same thing.*
Physically fights. Necessary to survive in poverty. Only knows the language of survival. Does not have language or belief system to use conflict resolution. Sees himself as less than a man if does not fight.	*Stress that fighting is unacceptable in school. Examine other options the student could live with at school. One option is not to settle the business at school.*
Hands always on someone else. Poverty has a heavy reliance on nonverbal data and touch.	*Allow them to draw or doodle. Have them hold their hands behind their backs when in line or standing. Give them as much to do with their hands as possible in a constructive way.*
Cannot follow directions. Little procedural memory used in poverty. Sequence not used or valued.	*Write steps on the board. Have them write at the top of the paper the steps needed to finish the task. Have them practice procedural self-talk.*
Extremely disorganized. Lack of planning, scheduling or prioritizing skills. Not taught in poverty. Also, probably does not have a place to put things at home so they can be found.	*Teach a simple color-coded method of organization in the classroom. Use the five-finger method for memory at the end of the day. Make students give a plan for their own organization.*
Only completed part of a task. No procedural self talk. Does not "see" the whole task.	*Write on the board all the parts of the task. Make students check off each part when finished.*
Disrespectful to teacher. Has lack of respect for authority and the system. May not know any adults worthy of respect.	*Tell students that approach is not a choice. Identify for students the correct voice tone and word choice that is acceptable. Make them practice.*
Harms other students, verbally or physically. This may be a way of life. Probably a way to buy space or distance. May have become a habitual response. Poverty tends to address issues in the negative.	*Tell the students that approach is not a choice. Have the students generate other options. Give students alternative verbal phrases.*
Cheats or steals. Indicative of weak support system, weak role models/emotional resources. May indicate extreme financial need. May indicate no instruction/guidance during formative years.	*Use metaphor story to find the reason or need the cheating and stealing met. Address the reason or need. Stress that the behavior is illegal and not a choice at school.*
Constantly talks. Poverty is very participatory.	*Make students write all questions and responses on a note card two days a week. Tell students they get five comments a day. Build participatory activities into the lesson.*

page 2

aha! aha! aha! aha! aha! aha! aha! aha! aha! aha! aha! aha! aha! aha! aha! aha! aha! aha!

Ruby K. Payne, Ph.D.   Poverty Series   Part III

access to another way to deal with the situation. For example, if I slam my finger in the car door, I can cry, cuss, hit the car, be silent, kick the tire, laugh, stoically open the car door, groan, etc.

The Language of Negotiation

One of the bigger issues with students from poverty is that many of them are their own parents. They parent themselves and others – often younger siblings. In many instances, they are the parent to the adult in the household.

Inside everyone's head are internal voices that guide the individual. These three voices are referred to as the child voice, the adult voice and the parent voice. It has been my observation that individuals who have become their own parent quite young do not have an internal adult voice. They have a child voice and a parent voice, but not an adult voice.

What an internal adult voice does is allow for negotiation. This voice provides the language of negotiation and allows the issues to be examined in a non-threatening way.

Educators tend to speak to students in a parent voice, particularly in discipline situations. To the student who is already functioning as a parent, this is unbearable, and almost immediately, the incident is exacerbated beyond the original happening. The tendency is for educators to also use the parent voice with poor parents because the assumption is that a lack of resources must indicate a lack of intelligence. Poor parents are extremely offended by this as well.

When the parent voice is used with a student who is already a parent in many ways, the outcome is anger. The student is angry because anger is based on fear. What the parent voice forces the student to do is either use the child voice or use the parent voice. If the student uses the parent voice, the student will get in trouble. If the student uses the child

---

**Educators tend to speak to students in a parent voice, particularly in discipline situations.
To the student who is already functioning as a parent, this is unbearable, and almost immediately, the incident is exacerbated beyond the original happening.**

---

voice, he or she will feel helpless and therefore at the mercy of the adult. Many students choose to use the parent voice in return because it is less frightening than the memories connected with being helpless.

Part of the reality of poverty is the language of survival. There are simply not enough resources to engage in a discussion of them. For example, if there are five hot dogs and five people, the distribution of the food is fairly clear. The condiments for the hot dogs are going to be limited so the discussion will be fairly limited as well. So the ability to see options and to negotiate among those options is not well developed. Contrast that, for example, with a middle class household where the discussion will be about how many hot dogs, what should go on the hot dog, etc.

To teach students to use the "language of negotiation," one must first teach them the phrases they can use. Especially, beginning in grade four, have them use the "adult" voice in discussions. Direct teach the notion of an adult voice and give them phrases to use. Make them tally each time they use a phrase from the "adult" voice. There will be laughter. However, over time, if teachers also model that voice in their interactions with students, they will hear more of those kinds of questions and statements.

In addition to this, several staff development programs are available to teach peer negotiation as well. It is important that as a part of the negotiation, the culture of origin is not

denigrated, but rather the ability to negotiate is seen as a survival skill for the work and school setting.

CHILD VOICE

Defensive, victimized, emotional, whining, lose mentality, strong negative non-verbal.

Quit picking on me. You don't love me. You want me to leave. Nobody likes (loves) me. I hate you. You are ugly. You make me sick. It's your fault. Don't blame me. She/he did it. You make me mad. You made me do it.

The child voice is also playful, spontaneous, curious, etc. The phrases listed occur in conflict or manipulative situations and impede resolution.

ADULT VOICE

Non-judgmental, free of negative. non-verbal, factual, often in question format, attitude of win-win.

In what ways could this be resolved? What criteria will be used to determine the effectiveness and quality of ... I would like to recommend ... What are the choices in this situation? I am comfortable (uncomfortable) with ... Options that could be considered are ... For me to be comfortable. I need the following things to occur ... These are the consequences of that choice or action ... We agree to disagree.

PARENT VOICE

Authoritative, directive, judgmental, evaluative, win-lose mentality, advising, (sometimes threatening, demanding, punitive).

page 3

10 Actions to Educate Students

You should not (should) do that. It is wrong (right) to do that. I would advise you to … That's stupid, immature, out of line, ridiculous. Life's not fair. Get busy. You are good, bad, worthless, beautiful (any judgmental, evaluative comment). You do as I say. If you weren't so …, this wouldn't happen to you.

The parent voice can also be very loving and supportive. These phrases listed occur during conflict and impede resolution. The internal parent voice can create shame and guilt.

Using Metaphor Stories

Another technique for working with students and adults is to use a metaphor story. A metaphor story will help an individual voice issues that affect their actions.

A metaphor story does not have any proper names in it. For example, a student keeps going to the nurse's office two or three times a week. There is nothing wrong with her, yet she keeps going.

Adult to Jennifer, the girl: "Jennifer, I am going to tell a story and I need you to help me. It is about a fourth-grade girl much like yourself. I need you to help me tell the story because I am not in the fourth grade. Once upon a time, there was a girl who went to the nurse's office. Why did the girl go to the nurse's office? *(Because she thought there was something wrong with her.)* So the girl went to the nurse's office because she thought there was something wrong with her. Did the nurse find anything wrong with her. *(No, the nurse did not.)* So the nurse did not find anything wrong with her, yet the girl kept going to the nurse. Why

did the girl keep going to the nurse? *(Because she thought there was something wrong with her.)* So the girl thought something was wrong with her. Why did the girl think there was something wrong with her? *(She saw a TV show …)*"

The story continues until the reason for the behavior is found and then the story needs to end on a positive note. "So, she went to the doctor, and he gave her tests and found that she was OK."

This is an actual case. What came out in the story was that Jennifer had seen a TV show in which a girl her age had died suddenly and had never known she was ill. Jennifer's parents took her to the doctor. He ran tests and told her she was fine. She did not go to the nurse's office anymore.

A metaphor story is to be used one-on-one when there is a need to understand the behavior and what is needed is to move the student to the appropriate behavior.

Teaching Hidden Rules

For example, if a student from poverty laughs when he/she is disciplined, the teacher needs to say, "Do you use the same rules to play all video games: No, you don't because you would lose. The same is true at school. There are street rules and there are school rules. Each set of rules helps you be successful where you are. So, at school, laughing when disciplined is not a choice. It does not help you to be successful. It only buys you more trouble. Keep a straight face and look contrite, even if you aren't."

That is an example of teaching a hidden rule. It can even be more straight forward with older students.

"Look, there are hidden rules on the street and hidden rules at school. What are they?" And then after the discussion, detail the rules that make the student successful where they are.

What Does This Information Mean in the School or Work Setting?

♦ Students from poverty need to have at least two sets of behaviors from which to choose – one set for the streets, and one set for school and work.

♦ The purpose of discipline should be to promote successful behaviors at school.

♦ Teaching students to use the adult voice, i.e. the language of negotiation, is important for their success in and out of school and can become an alternative to physical aggression.

♦ Structure and choice need to be a part of the discipline approach.

♦ Discipline should be a form of instruction.

Previously printed in *Instructional Leader* magazine.

Ruby K. Payne, Ph.D., founder and president of aha! Process, Inc. (1994), with more than 30 years experience as a professional educator, has been sharing her insights about the impact of poverty – and how to help educators and other professionals work effectively with individuals from poverty – in more than a thousand workshop settings through North America, Canada, and Australia.

More information on her book, *A Framework for Understanding Poverty*, can be found on her website, www.ahaprocess.com.

Students from poverty need to have at least two sets of behaviors from which to choose— one set for the streets, and one set for school and work.

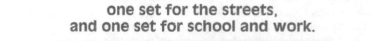

Reframing

> Reframing uses the adult voice to view the situation differently so that the desired behavior is compatible with the student's identity.
>
> Reframing doesn't work if the individual has a biochemical issue or an addiction.

10 Actions to Educate Students

9. Family Structure and Function

Understand the family resources and dynamics.

Why?

To better understand the resources the child has access to and better select interventions.

Family structure is the configuration of the relationship.

Family function is the extent to which a child is cared for and nurtured.

Family structure: two-parent families	Percentage of U.S. 6- to 11-year-olds in each type
Nuclear family	54%
Stepparent	9%
Adoptive family	2%
Grandparents alone	2%
Two same-sex parents	<1%

Family structure: single-parent families	Percentage of U.S. 6- to 11-year-olds in each type
Single mother (never married)	10%
Single mother (divorced, separated, or widowed)	13%
Grandparent alone	1%
Single father	4%

Family structure: more than two adults	Percentage of U.S. 6- to 11-year-olds in each type
Extended family	5%
Polygamous *	0%

* In some nations (not the United States), men can legally have several wives.

Note. Estimated from 2010 data in U.S. Bureau of the Census, Statistical Abstract and Current Population Reports: America's Families and Living Arrangements, 2009.

Note. From *The Developing Person Through the Life Span,* 8th ed., by K. S. Berger, 2010.

10 Actions to Educate Students

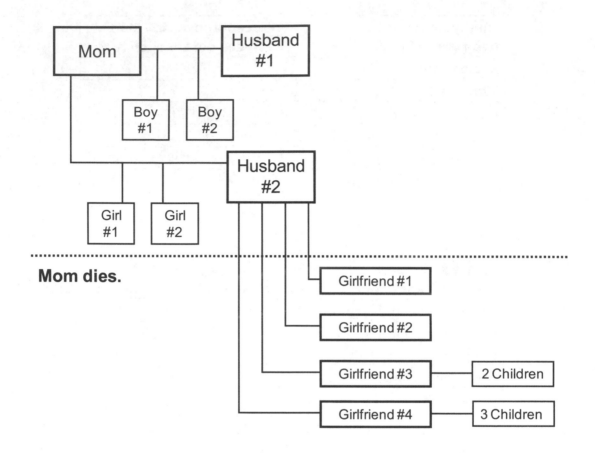

Mom dies.

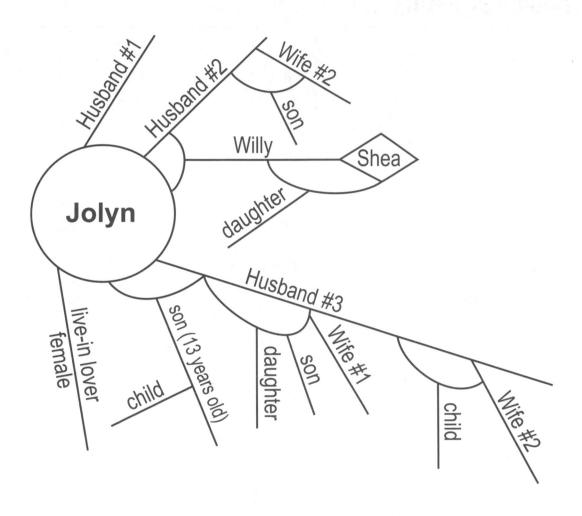

Draw Your Family Structure

Questions for Discussion

1. Who helped you with your homework?
2. Whom did you care about most? Who cared about you?
3. Were relationships competitive? Cooperative? Both?
4. Whom did you trust?
5. What did you think about authority?
6. What did you learn about relationships?

10 Actions to Educate Students

10. Questioning

Teach how to ask questions.

Why?

So students can get past the third-grade reading level—and so they can get inside their head and know what they know and what they don't know.

WRITING MULTIPLE-CHOICE QUESTIONS

Question:

a.
b.
c.
d.

Three Rules:

1. One wrong-answer choice must be funny.
2. Only one answer choice can be right.
3. May not use "all of the above," "none of the above," etc.

MATH QUESTIONS

1. Stems (see explanation below) need to use the terminology.

2. Distracters are:
   - Incorrect operation
   - Incorrect order
   - Decimal in wrong place
   - Answer in wrong form (percentage instead of number, etc.)
   - Missed step
   - Unnecessary information included
   - Computational errors

Note. From *Research-Based Strategies: Narrowing the Achievement Gap for Under-Resourced Students,* by Ruby K. Payne, 2010.

Questioning for Quality Thinking

REMEMBER: *Identification and recall of information*
Who, what, when, where, how _____?
Describe _____.

UNDERSTAND: *Organization and selection of facts and ideas*
Retell _____ in your own words.
What is the main idea of _____?

APPLY: *Use of facts, rules, principles*
How is _____ an example of _____?
How is _____ related to _____?
How does _____ compare/contrast with _____?

ANALYZE: *Separation of a whole into component parts*
What are the parts or features of _____?
Classify _____ according to _____.
How does _____ compare/contrast with _____?

CREATE: *Combination of ideas to form a new whole*
What would you predict/infer from _____?
What ideas would you add to _____?
How would you create/design a new _____?
What would happen if you combined _____ and _____?

EVALUATE: *Development of opinions, judgments, or decisions*
Do you agree with _____?
What do you think about _____?
What is the most important _____?
Prioritize _____ according to _____.
How would you decide about _____?
What criteria would you use to assess _____?

Source: *Adapted from Division of Instruction, Maryland State Department of Education*

10 Actions to Educate Students

10 Actions to Educate Students Checklist

	Action	Which do you already do?	Which of these will you add?
1	Build relationships of mutual respect.		
2	Teach students the hidden rules of school.		
3	Analyze the resources of your students, and make interventions based on resources the students have access to.		
4	Teach formal register, the language of school and work.		
5	Teach abstract processes.		
6	Teach mental models.		
7	Teach students how to plan.		
8	Use the adult voice and reframing to change behaviors.		
9	Understand the family resources and dynamics.		
10	Teach how to ask questions.		

Working with Parents
Building Relationships for Student Success

By Ruby K. Payne, Ph.D.

WORKING WITH STUDENTS' PARENTS AND GUARDIANS

Do not confuse having physical presence with parental involvement. The research seems to indicate that when a parent provides support, insistence, and expectations to the child, the presence or absence of a parent in the physical school building is immaterial. Therefore, training for parents should concentrate on these issues.

Think of parents not as a single group but as distinct sub-groups. For example:

1) career-oriented/too busy to attend school activities.
2) very involved in school activities.
3) single parents working two jobs/too busy to attend.
4) immigrant parents with language issues.
5) parents with overwhelming personal issues, such as addiction, illness, incarceration, evading the law.
6) surrogate parents: foster parents, grandparents, et al.
7) children who, in effect, are their own parents; they no longer have involved parents or guardians.

In your campus plan, identify specific ways you will target each group. Many discipline problems come from students whose parents are in sub-groups 5 and 7. These students desperately need relationships with adults that are long-term and stable. As a rule of thumb, the best (only?) way to make contact with groups 5 and 6 is through home visits, when and where possible. In sub-groups 5 and 7, the children/teens themselves are the de facto parents. Often they work full time in order to provide enough money for both the children and adults to survive. Time is a key issue for those students. It is unrealistic to treat parents as one group. The needs and issues are very different.

TIPS FOR WORKING WITH STUDENTS' PARENTS AND GUARDIANS

- Phone systems: Let parents and guardians talk to a real person. Phone systems at secondary schools often make it very difficult to talk to anyone.

- Have an awards assembly for parents.

- Identify a clear mechanism for getting information. For affluent parents, a Website is wonderful. For all parents, videos work. The videos need to be short and focused. For example, how to talk to your teenager, how to find out what is happening at the high school, how to get your child back to school after a suspension, etc.

- Another option is a predictable newsletter. But it needs to be simple, clear, and to the point—and it must include many icons or visuals so that it can be used whether you're literate or extremely busy. These newsletters can be posted outside the building in glass cases and updated weekly. They can be posted in supermarkets,

Laundromats, etc. The National Honor Society could take it on as a service project. Newsletters can be mailed home, a better option than children carrying them home.

- Pay parents to come in and call other parents. Have a list of things to say and have two rules: You may not discuss teachers and you may not discuss students other than your own children.

- Have gatherings that involve food. For example, anyone can come to the school for 50-cent hot dogs.

- If you do parenting classes, don't call them that. Focus on the student: "How to help your child …" Many parents of teenagers are desperate for good information about teens. Teenagers are typically tight-lipped and, unless you have much opportunity to be around them, as a parent you may not even know what is "normal." Find ways for individuals with lots of exposure to teenagers to share that information with parents and guardians.

- Adopt a plot of land to keep landscaped and clean. One school in a very poor neighborhood did this. Parents took pride in it. (Some even planted tomatoes!)

- Divide parents up among all the staff members (secretaries included). Each staff member contacts those parents and tells them, "If you have a question you cannot get an answer to, you can always call me."

- Create emotional safety for parents by being respectful of their concerns, openly sharing school activities, clarifying behavioral parameters/expectations of the school, and identifying available opportunities.

- For all activities, organizations, handbooks, etc., use simpler formats for giving the information. Liberally use visuals to appeal to the illiterate, the immigrant, and the busy.

WORKING WITH PARENTS FROM POVERTY

The first issue to address when working with parents from poverty is mutual respect. The second is the use of casual register. The third is the way discipline is used in the household. The fourth is the way time is viewed. And the fifth is the role of school and education in their lives.

First, for many parents in generational poverty, school is not given a high priority. It is often feared and resented. Their own personal experience may not have been positive, and school is alternately viewed as a babysitter or a necessary evil (i.e., "If I don't send my child, I will have to go to court"). Second, when parents come in, because of their heavy reliance on a win/lose approach to conflict, they may begin with an in-your-face approach. Remember, they are doing this, consciously or unconsciously, as a show of strength. Just stay in the adult voice. Use language that is clear and straightforward. If you use "educationese," they're likely to think you're trying to cheat or trick them.

Use these kinds of phrases with parents from poverty (these are the types of comments they often use with their own children):

- "Learning this will help your child win more often."

- "The mind is a mental weapon that no one can take from you."

- "If you do this, your child will be smarter and won't get cheated or tricked."

- "Learning this will help your child make more money."

- "This information will help keep your child safer."

- "I know you love and care about your child very much or you wouldn't be here" (but don't say this if you don't mean it).

Discipline in generational poverty vacillates from being very permissive to very punitive. The emotional mood of the moment often determines what occurs. Also, in some cultures, the approach to boys is very different from the approach to girls. When the discipline is highly punitive, there is often a belief system that (a) the harsher the punishment, the greater the forgiveness, and (b) the harsher punishment will make the young person stronger and tougher. Consequently, the notion of a systematic approach to discipline usually doesn't exist. There is rarely mediation or intervention about a behavior. Generally, it is a slap and a "Quit that." If guidance is being provided to the parent about behavior, use a WHAT, WHY, HOW approach with visuals. (See Ruby's comments at the end of this section on page 72, as well as a visual example of WHAT, WHY, HOW on page 74.)

GETTING PARENTS FROM POVERTY TO COME TO THE SCHOOL SETTING

One of the big difficulties for many schools is simply getting the parents into the school setting. Howard Johnson, a researcher at Southern Florida University, has done work with why urban parents come to school. The first reason they usually come is a crisis. What he has found is that rarely do they come to the school for reasons that school people think are important. So the first question that must be asked when trying to get parents to school is: "What's in it for the parents?"

A study done by the U.S. government in 1993 with Chapter 1 schools looked only at schools that were 75% or more low-income. Administrators of the study then identified students within those schools who achieved and students who did not. They developed a questionnaire looking at criteria in and out of school to understand the variables that made a difference in achievement. Interestingly, whether parents actually went to school or attended meetings at school was not a significant factor. What made the biggest difference was whether or not parents provided these three things for their children: support, insistence, and expectations.

SOME SUGGESTIONS (WHEN PARENTS FROM POVERTY COME TO THE SCHOOL)

1) Rather than the meeting format, use the museum format. That way parents can come and go when it's convenient for their schedule and their inclination. In other words, the school would be open from 6 to 9 p.m. Parents could come to one room to watch a video or a student performance. These would be repeated every 20 to 30 minutes. Another room could have a formal meeting at a given time. Another room could have board games for the students. Another room could have food.

2) Have food. Give gift certificates to grocery stores. These tend to be popular. Another favorite is clothesbaskets that have soap, shampoo, perfumes, etc., since food stamps don't always allow those purchases.

3) Let the children come with the parents—for several reasons. First, there often is jealousy or suspicion by the husband when his wife goes out alone. If the woman's children are with her, there is none. Second, school buildings tend to be big and confusing to parents. If the children go with them, the children help them find their way around. Third, a babysitter frequently isn't available. And fourth, children are natural icebreakers. Parents meet each other through their children.

4) Have classes that benefit parents. For example: how to speak English; how to fill out a job application; how to get a Social Security card; how to make money mowing yards, doing child care, baking, and repairing small engines. Also, schools can make their computer labs available on Saturdays to teach things like CAD (computer-aided design) and word processing—simple introductory courses that last four to five Saturdays for a couple of hours.

ALTERNATIVE APPROACHES

1) Use video. Virtually every home in poverty has a TV and a VCR or DVD player, even if it has very little else. Keep the videos under 15 minutes.
2) For all fliers home, use both verbal and visual information.
3) Provide simple, how-to activities that parents can do with children.

TIPS FOR WORKING WITH PARENTS FROM POVERTY

- Many adults from poverty didn't have a positive school experience. The greeting of the first staff member they encounter (secretary, aide, administrator, teacher) will either confirm their earlier experience or counter it. Some sort of building procedure and greeting should be agreed upon.

- Always call them by Mr. or Mrs. (unless told otherwise). It's a sign of respect.

- Identify your intent. Intent determines non-verbals. Parents from poverty decide if they like you based largely on your non-verbals. If they don't like you, they won't support you or work with you. For example, if your intent is to win, that will be reflected in your non-verbals. Likewise, if your intent is to understand, that will be reflected as well.

- Use humor (not sarcasm). They particularly look to see if you have a sense of humor about yourself. For example: Can you tell a story about yourself in which you weren't the hero? Can you poke fun at yourself?

- Deliver bad news through a story. If you state the bad news directly (e.g., your son was stealing), it will invite an automatic defense of the child. Instead, say, "Let me tell you a story. Maybe you can help me with the situation." Make sure you use the word story.

- If you're comfortable using casual register, use it. If not, don't use it. They'll probably think you're making fun of them.

- Be human and don't be afraid to indicate you don't have all the answers. As alluded to above, they distrust anyone who is "always the hero of his/her stories."

- Offer a cup of coffee. In poverty, coffee is frequently offered as a sign of welcome.

- Use the adult voice. Be understanding but firm. Be open to discussion, but don't change the consequences (unless new information surfaces or a better solution can be found).

- Be personally strong. You aren't respected in generational poverty unless you are personally strong. If you're threatened or have an in-your-face encounter, don't show fear. You don't need to be mean. Just don't show fear.

- If they're angry, they may appeal to physical power ("I'm going to beat you up!"). To calm them, say, "I know you love and care about your child very much or you wouldn't be here. What can we do that would show we also care?" Another phrase that often works is: "Are you mad at me, or are you just mad?"

- Use videos as a way to provide information and communicate with parents. Virtually every U.S. home in poverty has a TV, VCR, and DVD player. If possible, make the videos entertaining. They can be in any language, but they should be short.

- Story structure in generational poverty is episodic and random, and the discourse pattern is circular. Understand that these structures take much longer. Allow enough time during conferences for these structures to be used.

- Home visits by teachers are the fastest and easiest way to build a huge parent support base quickly. They also significantly reduce discipline issues. Use Title I money to pay teachers to make phone calls and do home visits before there is a problem. (The payoff from this one simple activity is tremendous.)

- Remember, the parents from poverty talked about you in the neighborhood before they came to see you. They often made outrageous comments about what they were going to say and do to you before they went to the school (entertainment is an important part of the culture of poverty). So when they return to the neighborhood, they have to report back. Some comments you may end up hearing will be so outrageous that they should be ignored. They were made because they told people in the neighborhood they were going to do so.

- As you discuss situations with parents, ask yourself what resources are available to these individuals. Some suggestions won't work because the resources simply aren't available.

- In middle class, when a topic is introduced that the individual doesn't want to discuss, he/she simply changes the subject. In generational poverty, the individual often tells the person what he/she wants to hear, particularly if that person is in a position of authority.

- Emphasize that there are two sets of rules: one set for school and work, another set for outside of school and work.

- Don't accept behaviors from adults that you don't accept from students.

TIPS FOR WORKING WITH PARENTS FROM WEALTH

- Don't use humor—at least initially—when discussing their child or situation. If you do, they'll think you don't care about them or their child.

- One of the hidden rules in affluence is: "It's not OK not to be perfect." So identifying your personal weaknesses will not appeal to them particularly. They want to know that you are very good at what you do. On the other hand, if you don't know something, don't try to bluff your way through. They will usually call your bluff.

- Another hidden rule in affluence is that you aren't respected unless you're able to discriminate by quality or artistic merit. Wealthy parents won't respect you unless you have expertise. If you aren't knowledgeable in a particular area,

read the experts or get a school district expert to sit in with you for the meeting.

- Don't use circular discourse or casual register. They want to get straight to the point and discuss the issue through formal register. They won't respect you if you waste their time.

- Do use the adult voice with affluent parents. Understand that they are skilled negotiators. Clearly establish parameters when discussing issues with them. Affluent parents often believe that they and their children don't need to follow or adhere to the "rules" of the organization. Be firm about those boundaries.

- Emphasize issues of safety, legal parameters, and the need for the student to develop coping mechanisms for greater success later in life.

- Understand that a primary motivator for wealthy parents is the financial, social, and academic success of their child. They're very interested in what you'll be able to do to help their child be successful.

- When affluent parents come to school and are upset, they likely will appeal to positional power, financial power, or connections ("I know the school board president" … "I'll call my lawyer" …). They also will attack the issues. Be prepared to articulate the issues, and use experts by name in the discussion.

- Don't be intimidated by the affluent parent. Do understand, regardless of your position, who is standing behind you to support you. If you have little or no support above you, make sure you don't paint yourself into a corner. Affluent parents will rattle the organizational "cage" in order to get what they want.

- Understand the competitive nature of wealth (especially among those with "new money") and the need to excel. Their children are expected to be the best. There tends to be disrespect for those in the service sector, including public service. However, if their child is happy and doing well, most of them will be incredibly supportive.

WORKING WITH PARENTS
OVERPROTECTIVE PARENTS

What is driving the protectiveness?

a. Child is a possession—defend your own no matter what they do.

b. Child is proof of parenting success—it's not OK not to be perfect.

c. Fear of loss—death, affection, loyalty.

d. Loss of another child—want to protect this child.

e. Change personal experience—"My mother never loved me."

f. Beliefs about parenting—"I just want to love him or her."

g. Emotional need of parent—loneliness, co-dependence, addiction.

Questions to ask

a. What is the very worst thing that could happen if we … ?

b. What is the very best thing that could happen if we … ?

c. What coping strategies could your child learn so that he or she could be more successful?

d. I know you love and care about your child very much. What can we do so that you know we love and care about him or her too?

e. Is there any evidence the fear is a reality?

f. How will this request help your child be more successful?

g. At what age will you allow your child to be responsible for his or her own actions?

Interventions

a. Reframing.

b. Using a story.

c. Establishing the parameters of school success.

d. Using other parents to establish perspective.

e. Establishing the parameters of parental interventions at school.

Appeals

Among affluent parents, an appeal to one of the following is effective: safety, expertise, legalities, or coping strategies to be more successful.

Among parents from poverty, an appeal to caring, winning, being smarter, or not getting cheated is effective.

CONFERENCING WITH PARENTS

A PROCESS

1. Stop the blackmail (if that is a part of the conference).

2. Listen. If needed, ask the parent to repeat the conversation and say this, "I am going to put this in writing and I want you to read back over it to see if I have gotten the main concerns. I will share this with the teacher and begin to work on this issue."

3. Pivot the conversation. Find out what the parent wants.

4. "Are you just mad or are you mad at me?"

5. "If you were queen or king, what would be your ideal solution to this?"

6. Establish the parameters, i.e. what the limitations of the situation are. (In some cases, you must get back with the parents after you have had a chance to find out the legal ramifications.)

7. Discuss options within those parameters.

8. Identify solutions.

9. Identify a plan. If necessary, put the plan in writing.

CASE STUDY: ANDREA

Andrea is a senior in high school. The counselor has come to you with a concern. It is the third six weeks of the first semester and Andrea is failing Algebra II honors. Andrea needs Algebra II to graduate. You call the parent in to look at the possibility of Andrea taking regular Algebra II so that she can get the credit and graduate. Algebra II is not offered as a part of summer school.

Andrea's mother comes in for the conference. She informs you in no uncertain terms that Andrea will not switch to an Algebra II regular class. Andrea is going to go to Texas A&M, all her friends are in that class, and she will not be switching. You explain to the mother that she will not have a diploma if she does not get a credit in Algebra II and that without a diploma she will not be admitted into A&M. The mother indicates that Andrea's grades are not the issue. Andrea's friends are the issue, and she is not going to approve the change.

- What is driving the parent behavior?
- What questions would you ask the parent?
- What intervention(s) would you make?

CASE STUDY: ANDY SLOCUM

Andy is in fourth grade. He is one of the youngest students in his class because he was barely 5 in first grade. You like Andy. Mrs. Slocum, his mother, is always at school. The family is very affluent, and Andy is her only child. The gossip network has it that Mrs. Slocum was married before and had two children and lost them in a custody battle.

Mrs. Slocum comes to you in March and tells you that she wants to retain Andy in the fourth grade. She knows he is gifted, but his grades aren't high enough to be in the program. He has been making A's and B's. She wants him to have all A's. From your observations, Andy is a bright child, he is somewhat immature (in comparison to his classmates), but he is very likable, has a winning personality, and is athletically gifted.

You tell Mrs. Slocum about the research regarding retention. The counselor has a conversation with Andy. You talk to the teacher about Mrs. Slocum's request, and the teacher is appalled. You tell Mrs. Slocum that you will not recommend retention. She tells you she will go to the superintendent if you don't recommend retention.

- What is driving the parent behavior?
- What questions would you ask the parent?
- What intervention(s) would you make?

CASE STUDY: CHARLES

You have a school that is 95% low-income, and at the fifth-grade level you have instituted a decision-making unit. Charles is in fifth grade, and his mother calls you one day and says the following:

"I heard that school was teaching decision making. My son ain't learnin' it. I want you to tell him that he has got to quit stealing so close to home. He needs to go three or four streets over. I don't know what that boy's problem is. That ain't no kind of decision making. If he can't make better decisions, I'm gonna tell the neighborhood about how your school ain't no good. And why they spendin' all that time on makin' decisions when he still don't know how to add?"

- What is driving the parent behavior?
- What questions would you ask the parent?
- What intervention(s) would you make?

CASE STUDY: MICHAEL

You are walking back to your office after visiting classrooms, and Mrs. Walker comes running in the front door. "What is wrong with Michael?" she asks. Michael is her son who's in third grade.

You say, "I haven't seen Michael this morning."

"Well, he just called and said that there is a problem. I need to talk to him."

Michael is called down to the office. During the conversation with his mother, it becomes apparent that Michael is angry with his teacher. He asked to get a drink of water, and instead went to the pay phone, called his mother, and told her to get up there right now. He's angry with his teacher because she gave an assignment he didn't want to do.

- What is driving the parent behavior?
- What questions would you ask the parent?
- What intervention(s) would you make?

CASE STUDY: MRS. SMITH

Mrs. Smith is a loud, gossiping parent who is active in the PTO. She has a son and a daughter. The son receives the focus of her attention. Yesterday Mrs. Smith called you because she is furious with you. She wants to know why you didn't do something about those students who put her fifth-grade son, Sam, in the trashcan at lunch. She tells you that if you don't do something about it, she will send her husband up there to "get you."

You aren't as concerned about that as you are that Mrs. Smith will go to the superintendent again with a badly skewed story.

You are surprised. The aides in the lunchroom are excellent, and you haven't heard anything about anyone being put in a trashcan. You talk to the fifth-grade teachers and the aides. No one heard anything about this, nor did they see anything.

So you call Sam in and talk to him. You ask for details about the incident—when, where, who. The details are very fuzzy: No, it wasn't during lunch, it was in the hall. He couldn't remember the names; they stuffed him in there before he could see them. You probe some more. Finally, Sam says, "Every

night when I go home my mom asks me what bad thing happened at school today. If I say nothing, she tells me I'm lying to her. So I decided to tell her I got put in a trashcan."

You recall incident after incident where Mom "rescues" Sam and threatens to send Dad up to see you if you don't do what she wants.

- What is driving the parent behavior?
- What questions would you ask the parent?
- What intervention(s) would you make?

CASE STUDY: MR. AND MRS. DESHOTELS

The second-grade teacher comes to you in January and tells you that Jacque has already had 25 absences this school year. The teacher has called Jacque's mother for an explanation, but the only explanation is that Jacque doesn't feel well. You look at her records for the year before; she had 36 absences in first grade.

You call the home and are unable to make contact. You get an answering machine. Finally, you send a letter, outlining the law about absences and stating your concern. You hear nothing. The next week, Jacque is absent another two days. You send a letter requesting a conference and indicate that if the absences continue without explanation, you will be required to take the next legal step.

You get a phone call from Mr. Deshotels. He cusses at you, tells you he will get a lawyer, etc. You find out from his monologue that he is a long-distance trucker, and you ask him if he knows how many absences his daughter has. He replies belligerently that he does. You say that you think 26 absences without a medical cause for one semester are excessive. Suddenly there is silence at the other end of the phone.

- What is driving the parent behavior?
- What questions would you ask the parent?
- What intervention(s) would you make?

CASE STUDY: MRS. BROWN

Mrs. Brown is a member of the Pentecostal Church, and she comes to see you about a novel that is being used in fourth grade. She is very upset that the school would have this book. The book is about a 12-year-old boy who goes on a hunt for a deer and comes to understand who he is. It's a book about coming of age and finding identity. She explains to you that the book is really not about a hunt, but the deer really represents a female and the book is about the sexual hunt. You tell her that the district has a choice option on books and that her daughter does not need to read the book; another book will be found for her daughter.

Mrs. Brown isn't satisfied and tells you that you don't understand. The book isn't suitable for any fourth-grader, says Mrs. Brown, and she will work long and hard to make sure it isn't read by anyone in fourth grade, adding that it's wrong to have a book like that in the schools. She has talked to her minister about it. Her minister is willing to go to a board meeting with her to protest the use of such inappropriate sexual reading in elementary school.

- What is driving the parent behavior?
- What questions would you ask the parent?
- What intervention(s) would you make?

A NOTE RUBY PAYNE RECEIVED FROM AN ASSISTANT PRINCIPAL

I attended the Train the Trainers session in Houston in July. It was great. At the time, I had no idea how useful it was going to be when I was placed as assistant principal for the first time.

I am having a hard time in this school because there is a problem I've never had to deal with. It sounds like something Ruby could shed some light on, but I don't remember her covering it at the session. A large number of parents in this school beat their children when I send a note or call home about the students' behaviors. I have had to call [child protective services] many days after punishing a child. Staff members at school are as overwhelmed as I am. They say this hasn't been a large problem until just recently. Many are holding back on sending students to the office because of fear of how the parents will handle the child afterward. All of us are anxious for some guidance. Can you give us some information or recommend some sources where we can do some reading? We pray for both Ruby and divine guidance. You can e-mail me here at school or at home.

RUBY'S RESPONSE

It was great to hear from you and know that the training was helpful.

About beating children. Yes, this is a very common response in generational poverty, particularly in Caucasian and African-American settings. It is not as much of a pattern in Hispanic generational poverty, unless there are multiple relationships.

There are several reasons why parents beat their children.

First, many times the parents have only two voices—a parent voice and a child voice. To move a child to self-governance, a person needs to have a third voice, an adult voice, so that the child can examine choices. Many parents cannot do this because they don't have an adult voice. So they use the parent voice. And in conflict, the parent voice tends to be a very harsh, punitive voice.

The second reason they beat their children is that typically they don't know any other approach. Usually raised themselves under punitive parenting, they believe the maxim that to spare the rod is to spoil the child.

The third reason is that it's part of the penance-forgiveness ritual. If you believe that you are fated, then you really cannot change your behavior. So the greater the penance, the greater the forgiveness. You will often find that after parents beat their children (penance) they engage in a ritual of forgiveness. Forgiveness can include any or all of the following: cooking them their favorite meal; permissiveness; and giving them alcohol, cigarettes, part of the drug stash, and money. Or a parent might even come to school and chew someone out just to show their child that he/she is forgiven. The thinking tends to be the following:

- I do the behavior because I am fated; I cannot change who I am.

- If I am fated, then I can't really change what I do.

- If I can't change what I do, then the real crime is getting caught.

- But if I get caught, then I am going to deny it.

- Because if I deny it, I might not get punished.

- However, if I do get punished, then I have also gotten forgiven.

- And I'm free to do the behavior again.

I have some suggestions for you.

First of all, I would approach the situation differently. When an incident occurs, I would call the parent and say, "I need your help. We are asking that you use a WHAT, WHY, HOW approach to discipline, which will help us here at school. That is what we are doing. When your child does something you don't like, please tell him WHAT he did, WHY that was not OK, and HOW to do it right. We want him to win every time and be smarter at school. So to help us, please use the WHAT, WHY, HOW approach. (As a reference point for yourself and parents, make a little brochure or paper with this approach clearly shown.) Then say, "Please do not hit him. When you hit him, we are required by law to call [child protective services]. We don't want to have to do that. So please help us."

Parents do what they believe to be the right thing. Some will say to you, "Honey, you do what you have to at school, and we'll do what we have to at home."

Then you say, "I know you love and care about your child very much or you wouldn't be taking the time to talk to me. But I need your help, and I know you don't want me to call [child protective services]. So, for anything having to do with your child and school, please use the WHAT, WHY, HOW approach. It's a simple 1-2-3 deal. It's not easy being a parent, and we want you to be able to win as a parent. So please help us."

For the parents with whom this doesn't work, I would not call home or send notes anymore. I would look more for positive reinforcements than negative reinforcements. There is nothing we can do at school that is as negative as some of the stuff that happens outside of school.

Please stay in touch, and let me know how things are going.

TO DISCIPLINE YOUR CHILD/STUDENT, USE THESE STEPS

1) **STOP** the behavior that is inappropriate.

2) Tell the child **WHAT** he/she did that was wrong.

3) Tell the child **WHY** the behavior was wrong and its consequences.

4) Tell the child **HOW** to behave the next time.

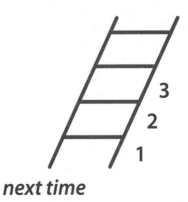

next time

Ruby K. Payne, Ph.D.

Parent and Community Involvement

By Ruby K. Payne, Ph.D.
Founder of aha! Process, Inc.

An integral part of a principal's role is working with parents. Conflicts that arise because of time constraints, differing belief systems, and difficult social and behavioral issues consume a large chunk of a principal's time. Furthermore, in almost all legislation, parental involvement is now either required or considered to be a key component in improving student achievement. So how does a principal get parental involvement?

First of all, some concepts need to be revisited. There is no correlation between the *physical presence* of parents at school and student achievement. The correlation is between student achievement and *parental involvement*. So getting parents to physically come to the school is not a key issue in student achievement.

Second, another concept that needs to be revisited is the "one size fits all" approach, which only works when the student population is very homogenous. It doesn't work when the student population is racially or socioeconomically diverse.

The third concept is that our current scheduling of parental activities is fine—and that all activities must involve the parent coming in to the school. The scheduling and structuring of parental outreach and activities is often set up for the convenience of school personnel, rather than the parents, and is one-way, i.e., school personnel do not go to the parents. That needs to change.

The fourth concept is that parents actually have a support system that allows them to participate in school activities and that their experience with school has been positive. For many parents this is simply not true.

And last but not least, a concept among school personnel is that many parents are difficult. Tools to address difficult parents give teachers and administrators more efficacy and, therefore, often more success.

New Model to Involve Parents

This article is going to provide a model that involves the following: (1) niche marketing to parents; (2) building a layered, "community of support" approach (Wehlage, et al., 1989; El Puente Project, 2003) involving myriad interventions and different scheduling; and (3) tools for dealing with difficult parents, parents from different economic classes, and parent/teacher conferences.

PART I: NICHE MARKETING TO PARENTS

Niche marketing is a term used in advertising. Simply put, it means that one size does not fit all and that marketing needs to be targeted at specific audiences. The following table outlines some of the subgroups of parents found in many schools and ideas for involvement in their child's education. *A parent does not need to come to school to be involved.*

Put these activities into the site-based plan so that they occur. The activities actually become a marketing plan for the campus.

SUBGROUPS OF PARENTS	IDEAS FOR INVOLVEMENT
Two-career parents	Put many things in print, e.g., fliers, newsletters, Web pages, etc. These parents will read and keep informed. Ask for e-mail addresses and send a monthly or weekly e-mail that updates them on the classroom and school activities.
Involved parents	These parents are at school, volunteering their help. The issue here is over involvement and parents wanting to take on administrative roles. Sometimes the boundaries involving student privacy need to be revisited.
Non-working and uninvolved parents	This occurs at both ends of the economic spectrum. Phone banks where parents call parents and tell them about school activities begins a network. Home contacts are very powerful, as are coffee klatches (see Part II for explanation).
Surrogate parents	These are grandparents, foster parents, etc. They often need emotional support. Assign them a mentor—e.g., a counselor or involved parent—who touches base with them once a month.

(Chart continues on page 2)

Readings

PART I: NICHE MARKETING TO PARENTS *(continued from page 1)*

SUBGROUPS OF PARENTS	IDEAS FOR INVOLVEMENT
Immigrant parents	Make short videos dubbed in their own language explaining how school works, how to talk to the teacher, what grades mean, what homework means, etc. Have the videos made by a person in your community from that immigrant group. DO NOT MAKE THEM TOO SLICK OR PROFESSIONAL because they will not be believed.
Parents working two jobs	Color-code the information you send home. White paper is "nice to know." Yellow paper indicates a concern. Red paper means that immediate attention is needed. You can call these parents at work as long as you do not talk at that time; ask them to call you back. Videos to introduce the teacher work well also.
Single parents	Structure activities that make life easier for the parent, activities that would include the children or child care, food (so they don't need to cook), or activities scheduled on the weekends or with open time frames rather than specific meeting times. Videos to introduce the teacher also work well here.
Parents who are unavailable and students who, in effect, are their own parents	These are parents who are incarcerated, mentally ill, physically ill, traveling a great deal, have been sent back to their native country, have an addiction, etc. Teach the student how to be his/her own parent and provide linkages for the student to other school service agencies. Have the counselor have "what if" lunches where pizza is brought in and four or five students in this position discuss issues.
Parents who are "crazymakers"	There are only a few of these in a building (less than 1%), but they can destroy time and energy. These are the parents who constantly have a complaint. Each time a solution is reached, there is a new complaint. School personnel need to take their daily rate, divide it by 8 to calculate an hourly rate, and document the cost of personnel time used by one parent. No board of education wants to know that one parent took $60,000 to $70,000 of personnel time for no reason.

A part of site-based planning is to identify the percentages of parents who fit into these categories. If you have many parents in one subgroup, then it would be important to address more of those involvement issues.

PART II: BUILDING COMMUNITIES OF SUPPORT

The layering and structuring of "practices that contribute to student engagement and high school completion" is the basic concept in communities of support. "Chief among these is the ability of school personnel to create communities of support that are concerned about how students perform and express that concern in genuine, effective, caring ways" (El Puente Project, 2003). So how does one do that? One way is to create a scaffolding of interventions. The other is by creating linkages to community groups.

The following suggestions can help create communities of support for parents:

a) Mutual respect: Parents are welcomed by first-line staff. Parents are welcome in the building. Accusatory and blaming language is not present.

b) School design teams: A cross-section of staff, parents, law enforcement, ministers, and students who identify issues of support.

c) Home contacts: These are not home visits but quick five-minute visits to the home at the beginning of school to say hello. Substitutes are used to release teachers to do this.

d) Videos: These can be made by the staff and students to introduce faculty, to tell about school discipline programs, to highlight upcoming events, etc.

e) Student and parent voices: Through informal conversation (not meetings), parents and students are asked what the school could do to better serve them.

f) Weekend activities: Friday evenings, Saturday mornings, and Sunday afternoons work the best.

g) Varied and targeted parental involvement activities: Free donuts for dads the first Monday of every month. Carnations for moms. Lunch for grandparents. Picnics for people who live in the student's house.

h) Support mechanisms for parents that involve follow-up: 3x5 cards with the steps that will be followed. Magnets for the refrigerator that list school phone numbers and holidays. Stickers that parents can give to the child for good behaviors.

i) Informal coffee klatches: Counselor or principal asks a parent with whom they already have a relationship to invite three or four other friends over for coffee in the parent's home. The principal or counselor brings the donuts. This is a forum for an informal discussion about what bothers parents, what they would like to see, what they like, etc.

page 2

Readings

j) Overcoming reluctance to participate by creating one-on-one relationships.

k) Tools for dealing with parent/teacher conferences.

l) Tools for dealing with difficult parents.

m) Simple written documents that have pictures and words and/or cartoons.

n) Using networking capabilities in the community: Make a flier with cartoons that is one page and has an advertisement for a business in the community on the back. Introduce your faculty through cartoons. The advertiser pays for the paper and the printing. Distribute them to beauty salons, grocery stores, barbershops, churches, etc., much like a local community shopper or merchandiser.

o) Information for parents that enhances their lives: Offer information like how to fix bad credit (knowledge about money), how to manage a difficult boss (conflict-resolution skills), etc.

p) Information on video or in cartoon that helps parents deal with their children, i.e., how to enhance obedience in your child.

q) Giving awards to parents: A child identifies something a parent has done. On a Saturday morning the child gives a certificate to his/her parent and thanks the parent.

r) Parent/teacher conferences led by the student.

s) Weekend activities that use the computers and athletic facilities of the campus.

t) Partner with a campus that has a surplus of parent involvement.

u) Peer-mediation training for students: They teach it to parents informally.

v) Teaching students to be better friends: Have students list the five friends they go to when they have a problem. Tally who are the "best friends." Teach them how to ask questions to solve problems. Teach them how to identify which problems are serious and need to be referred, such as threats of suicide.

w) Teaching parents to be better friends to other adults.

x) Block parties: Get a street blocked off for an afternoon and have a party.

In other words, creating communities of support is a layered, varied set of interventions and activities. The idea that a school can have X number of meetings a year, a carnival, and a Halloween party is not enough. What must occur is a scaffolding of interventions.

PART III: TOOLS TO USE FOR PARENT/TEACHER CONFERENCES AND DEALING WITH DIFFICULT PARENTS

School personnel need to hone their conferencing skills to create a supportive environment for parents and develop conflict-resolution skills to deal more effectively with difficult parents. Our online questionnaires for new teachers have found that their two greatest issues are student discipline and dealing with parents.

Outlined below is a step sheet for the process to be used as a part of the parent/teacher conference, a parent/teacher conferencing form (page 5), questions to ask to facilitate resolution of conflicts, and phrases to use by economic group.

Step Sheet for Parent/Teacher Conferences

1. Contact the parent. If it's going to be a difficult conference, have the principal or a counselor attend.

2. Make a list of items that need to be in the folder that is shared with parents: student work, grades, discipline referrals, rubrics, tests, etc.

3. If time is short, let the parent know about that and apologize for the time frame.

4. Have mutual respect for the parent. Ask the parent to tell you about his/her child. "As we begin this conversation, what would you like me to know about Johnny? You love him and care about him or you would not have come to see me." They know more about the child than you do. Tap into that knowledge. Do not use "why" questions. Say "our child." (See below for questions to ask.)

5. Keep the conference focused on the data and the issues. "I have a folder of John's work. I would like to go through the folder with you and talk about his work." Or, if the student is there, "John is going to go through the folder and show you his work." Let the work speak for itself.

6. Ask the parent if he/she has questions.

7. Identify the follow-up strategies and tools to be used.

8. Thank the parent for coming.

Questions/Techniques to Facilitate the Conference

1. Stay away from "why" questions. Instead, begin with these words: *when, how, what, which.* For example: "When he did that, what did he want? How will that help him be more successful? How will

that help him win? What have you noticed? How would you like to do the follow-up? Which way would work best for you? What is the worst-case scenario? What is the best-case scenario? How would you like to have this resolved? What plan could we use?"

2. STAY AWAY FROM STATEMENTS. Use data and questions.

3. Identify the fuzzy nouns and pronouns (*everyone, they, them, all the parents, all the students, women, men, kids, etc.*). If those words are in the conversation, ask this question: "Specifically who or which ...?"

4. Identify vague qualifiers. Example: "It's better." ("Better than what?")

5. Identify fuzzy adverbs. Example: "He/she always has a bad teacher." ("Always? Has there ever been a time when the teacher was good?")

6. Identify the emotion in a statement. For example: "You're racist!" ("I sense that you feel the school is unfair and insensitive. Can you give me a specific example that would help me understand?")

7. Identify the hidden rules or beliefs (*should, must, can't, have to, ought to, should not, mandatory*). Example: "What would happen if you did? What stops you?"

8. Identify the parameters of the school. Example: "We do that to keep children safe." Or: "Just as we don't allow other parents to come in and tell us what to do with your child, we cannot allow you to dictate procedure for other people's children."

Phrases to Use with Parents

IN POVERTY	IN AFFLUENCE
This will help him/her win more often.	This coping strategy will help him/her be more successful in the corporate world.
This will keep him/her from being cheated.	Responsibility and decision making are learned behaviors. We can give him/her the competitive edge as an adult by learning these behaviors now.
This will help him/her be respected and in control.	This will keep him/her safe.
This will help him/her be tougher and stronger.	This will help him/her have the advantage.
His/her mind is a tool and a weapon that no one can take away.	This is a legal requirement.
This will help him/her be smarter.	This is an investment in your child's future success.
This will help keep you safe when you are old.	He/she will need processes/skills/content in the work world.
This is a legal requirement.	
I know that you love and care about your child very much or you would not have come to see me.	

CONCLUSION

The concepts that schools have used for so long to involve parents tend to be one-way, linear, and meeting-oriented. Just as advertisers have discovered that multiple messages and mediums are required to influence buyers, we must also use the scaffolding of relationships, interventions, activities, mutual respect, conflict resolution, and targeted assistance to create communities of support.

BIBLIOGRAPHY

Rosario, Jose R. (2003). *Final Narrative Report: September 1, 2002-August 31, 2003*. Hispanic Education Center, El Puente Project. Indianapolis, IN. Funded by Lumina Foundation for Education.

Wehlage, G.G., Rutter, R.A., Smith, G.A., Lesko, N., & Fernandez, R.R. (1989). *Reducing the Risk: Schools as Communities of Support*. Philadelphia, PA: Falmer Press.

Ruby K. Payne, Ph.D., founder of **aha!** Process, Inc. (1994), with more than 30 years experience as a professional educator, has been sharing her insights about the impact of poverty — and how to help educators and other professionals work effectively with individuals from poverty—in more than a thousand workshop settings through North America, Canada, and Australia.

Her seminal work, *A Framework for Understanding Poverty,* teaches the hidden rules of economic class and spreads the message that, despite the obstacles poverty can create in all types of interaction, there are specific strategies for overcoming them. Since publishing *Framework* in 1995, Dr. Payne also has written or co-authored nearly a dozen books surrounding these issues in such areas as education, social services, the workplace, faith communities, and leadership.

More information on her book, *A Framework for Understanding Poverty,* can be found on her website, www.ahaprocess.com.

PARENT/TEACHER CONFERENCE FORM WITH STUDENT

Student name_____ Date_____ Time_____

Parent name_____ Teacher_____

PURPOSE OF THE CONFERENCE (CHECK AS MANY AS APPLY)

_____ scheduled teacher/parent conference

_____ student achievement issue

_____ parent-initiated

_____ discipline issue

_____ social/emotional issue

WHAT IS THE DESIRED GOAL OF THE CONFERENCE?

WHAT DATA WILL I OR THE STUDENT SHOW THE PARENT? Student work, discipline referrals, student planning documents?

WHAT QUESTIONS NEED TO BE ASKED? WHAT ISSUES NEED TO BE DISCUSSED?

WHAT FOLLOW-UP TOOLS AND STRATEGIES WILL BE IDENTIFIED?

Toward a Cognitive Model for Better Understanding Socioeconomic Class

By Ruby K. Payne, Ph.D.

ONE OF THE PERSISTENT DEBATES in social-stratification research and theory pertains to the causation of both poverty and wealth. In fact, four prevalent theories are extant: individual choice, exploitation/colonialism, economic and social systems, and resources of a community. I would suggest a fifth explanation: the cognition and knowledge base of the individual and his/her relationships.

All disciplines move through three research stages: classification, correlation, and causation. For example, when people first saw the stars, they named them and called it astrology. Then Galileo came along and said the stars moved in relationship to each other and called that astronomy. And then Newton appeared and said there is a reason they do that and called it gravity. In social theory, however, there is no clear agreement about what causes social class.

Most legislation in the United States the last 70 years has been based on social determinism. In the 1800s, Western civilization tended to believe in genetic determinism. Who you were and what could happen to you were based largely on your genetic inheritance. Then the women's movement and the civil-rights movement came along and said it didn't matter what you were born with. If you aren't allowed to vote, own property, or be educated, then your genes were essentially a moot point. This is called social determinism. It's "the system" that holds you back. Beginning in the 1940s, we began to look at artificial intelligence, brain and MRI scans, and eventually computer programming. We became very interested in how individuals process and manipulate information and knowledge. It would seem it is time for a cognitive model of social class. In other words, what thinking and knowledge are necessary to function in different social-class environments? How can individual initiative—based on resources—overcome, even transcend, the very real impact of social determinism?

Social determinism is based on correlation models that use numbers as their main point of proof. In cognitive models of brain processing, the brain tends to process in patterns. As a person has greater expertise in a situation or discipline, he/she processes very rapidly in patterns (Gladwell, 2005; Bloom, 1976). So a cognitive model would rely more heavily on patterns of thinking as evidenced in patterns of behaviors. Many researchers are uncomfortable looking at patterns and would prefer the "safety" and proof of numbers. Yet experts in any discipline would agree that there are patterns of response among human beings.

Social determinism cannot answer the following questions:

- Why do only 42% of children born to parents in the bottom quintile stay in the bottom quintile? (Isaacs, 2007)

- Why do only 36% of the children born to households in the top quintile stay there?

- Why do 7% of individuals make it from the bottom 20% of household to the top 20% of households?

- Why are 75% of the Forbes list of the 400 wealthiest people in America new money?

- Why is there such a "great divide" in income by educational attainment?

And we know that there are correlates for poverty to the non-dominant race, to female gender, to disability, and to youth. However, if it were just about race, then whites wouldn't comprise 58% of the people in poverty in the United States (U.S. Census, 2000). And if poverty were just about female gender, then 75% of first-time prisoners wouldn't be uneducated males from poverty.

There must be additional causations. I will argue that there is a relationship between the demands of the environment, the resources one has, and the knowledge base one has.

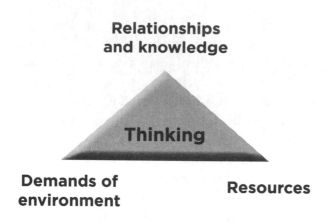

The Correlation Between Knowledge and What You Spend Your Time Doing

Knowledge is a huge form of privilege. How you spend your time determines to a large extent your knowledge base—and vice versa. In our research with individuals in poverty, this (see chart below) is what they say they spend their time on:

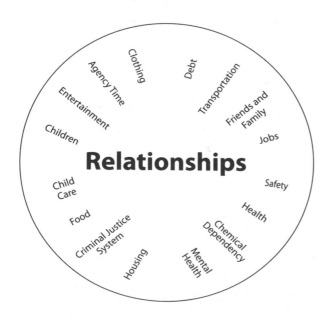

Developed by Philip DeVol (2006)

This is what people in middle class (which we define as stability of resources—not just about money) say they spend their time on:

Developed by Philip DeVol (2006)

This is what people in wealth say they spend their time on:

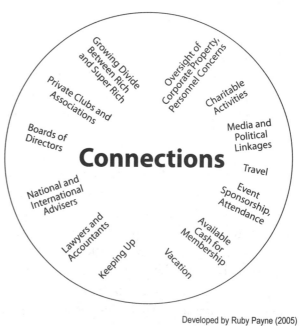

Developed by Ruby Payne (2005)

Just as social access, money, and being a member of the dominant group constitute forms of privilege, so is knowledge.

Resourced and Under-Resourced

Some individuals don't like the terminology of poverty, middle class, and wealth. Then let us use the terms resourced and under-resourced. There are correlates that tend to occur as a person has fewer or greater resources.

UNDER-RESOURCED		RESOURCED
Instability/crisis	. . . .	Stability
Isolation	. . . .	Exposure
Dysfunction	. . . .	Functionality
Concrete reality	. . . .	Abstract representational reality
Casual, oral language	. . . .	Written, formal register
Thought polarization	. . . .	Option seeking
Survival	. . . .	Abundance
No work/intermittent work	. . . .	Work/careers/larger cause
Poverty	. . . .	Wealth
Less educated	. . . .	More educated

Resources that bring stability include the following:

FINANCIAL
Having the money to purchase goods and services.

EMOTIONAL
Being able to choose and control emotional responses, particularly to negative situations, without engaging in self-destructive behavior. This is an internal resource and shows itself through stamina, perseverance, and choices.

MENTAL
Having the mental abilities and acquired skills (reading, writing, computing) to deal with daily life.

SPIRITUAL
Believing in divine purpose and guidance.

PHYSICAL
Having physical health and mobility.

SUPPORT SYSTEMS
Having friends, family, and backup resources available to access in times of need. These are external resources.

RELATIONSHIPS/ROLE MODELS
Having frequent access to adult(s) who are appropriate, who are nurturing, and who do not engage in self-destructive behavior.

KNOWLEDGE OF HIDDEN RULES
Knowing the unspoken cues and habits of a group.

LANGUAGE/FORMAL REGISTER
Having the vocabulary, language ability, and negotiation skills necessary to succeed in school and/or work settings.

Research Examples of the Frame of Environmental Demands, Relationships, and Knowledge

In a study after Hurricane Katrina hit New Orleans, it was found that the people in poverty who made it out of poor neighborhoods had more social capital than the people in poverty who didn't make it out.

Chicago researchers (Berliner, 2009) found that "neighborhood efficacy" or lack thereof did more to impact student achievement than the family did. So the "thinking" and the mindset of the environment are a huge factor in behavior.

We know from research in Australia (Najman et al., 2004) that the verbal comprehension scores of 5-year-olds and the non-verbal reasoning scores of 14-year-olds was significantly correlated to the maternal grandfather's occupation. So the combination of knowledge base and learning environment in a family system over the generations also plays a key role in the potential of young people.

Conclusion

For most of the last 70 years U.S. legislators have used a compliance model based on social determinism in an attempt to eradicate poverty. It simply hasn't worked. Isn't it time to consider additional causations and explanations? If you only give individuals resources but don't give them the capacity to develop those resources, then a government creates a group of individuals who cannot develop their own resource base. This is not a sustainable model. The role of knowledge in creating resources cannot be underestimated. It must be incorporated into a better understanding of class structures—and how they develop—in the United States.

References

Berliner, D. C. (2009). Poverty and potential: Out-of-school factors and school success. Boulder: National Educational Policy Center. Retrieved from http://epicpolicy.org/publication/poverty-and-potential

Bloom, B. (1976). Human characteristics and school learning. New York, NY: McGraw-Hill.

Forbes 400 richest Americans. (2011). New York, NY: Forbes.com LLC. Retrieved from http://www.forbes.com/wealth/forbes-400

Gladwell, M. (2005). Blink: The power of thinking without thinking. New York, NY: Little, Brown.

Isaacs, J. B. (2007). Economic mobility across generations. Economic Mobility Project, Pew Charitable Trusts. Retrieved from http://www.pewtrusts.org/uploadedFiles/wwwpewtrustsorg/Reports/Economic_Mobility/EMP%20 Across%20Generations%20ES%20+%20Chapter.pdf

Najman, J. M., Aird, R., Bor, W., O'Callaghan, M., Williams, G. M., & Shuttlewood, G. J. (2004). The generational transmission of socioeconomic inequalities in child cognitive development and emotional health. Social Science and Medicine, 58(6), 1147–1158. doi:10.1016/S0277-9536(03)00286-7

U.S. Bureau of the Census. (2000). www.census.gov

Note. From *From Understanding Poverty to Building Human Capacity,* by Ruby K. Payne, 2012.

What Information Does *A Framework for Understanding Poverty* Have That Cannot Be Obtained Easily from Other Sources?

Why Do Critics Love to Hate It and Practitioners Love to Use It?

By Ruby K. Payne, Ph.D.

W HAT IS IT THAT MAKES *A Framework for Understanding Poverty* (Payne, 2005) so widely embraced and used by practitioners? Some critics attribute the popularity to the bias of the readers. But that hardly makes sense because so many educators are the first generation to be college-educated in their families. Many of their parents came from poverty, so the information resonates with them. Therefore, what actually does the work offer that individuals cannot get from other sources?

Most studies of class issues are statistical or descriptive and use one of four frames of reference to identify what causes class. These four frames are:

- Individual choices
- Resources of the community
- Racial/gender exploitation
- Economic/political systems and structures.

Most current studies describe poverty as a systemic problem involving racial/gender exploitation. Yes, this is a significant contributor to poverty. Such a *sole* approach, however, does not answer this question: If the system is to blame, why do some people make it out and others never do? Thirty percent of Americans born in the bottom quintile make it out of that quintile (Isaacs, Sawhill, & Haskins, n.d.). And furthermore, why is it that the first waves of political refugees who have come to United States in abject poverty usually have re-created, within one generation, the asset base they left behind? They make it out because of human capital. Ignorance is just as oppressive as any systemic barrier. Human capital is developed through education, employment, the intergenerational transfer of knowledge, and social bridging capital. Money makes human capital development easier, but money alone does not develop human capital. Furthermore, any system in the world will oppress you if you are uneducated and unemployed.

This analysis of class is a cognitive approach based upon a 32-year longitudinal study of living next to and in a poverty neighborhood of mostly whites. It examines the thinking that comes from the "situated learning" environment of generational poverty (Lave & Wenger, 1991). It is the accumulation of years of living with and next to this situated learning environment. The book does not assign moral value to the thinking or the behaviors but rather says, These are patterns that you see. These are why individuals use these patterns, and here is what you can do to help those individuals make the transition to the "decontextualized" environment of formal schooling, if they so desire to make that transition.

In the book *Change or Die,* Deutschman (2007) says that for people to change, three things must happen. They must relate, reframe, and repeat. And that is precisely what the Framework book does: It identifies what one must to do develop relationships, what must be reframed to go from poverty to the decontextualized world of formal schooling, and the skills and behaviors that must be repeated in order to do that. And whether one likes it or not, both schools and social agencies have as their bottom line: *change.* That is what they are getting paid to do.

Again, not everyone wants to change. The question is this: Do you have a choice not to live in poverty? If you are not educated or employed, then choice has been taken from you.

So what is it about the book that is so important to practitioners? Why do so many practitioners love to use it?

1. A language to talk about the experience of generational poverty

In order to reframe anything, one must have language to do that. You must have language to talk about your current experience and the experience to which you are moving. Class, just like race, is experienced at a very personal level first and impacts thinking (Lave & Wenger, 1991). The book explains the patterns in the situated learning environment of generational poverty and is very careful to say that not everyone will have those patterns. As one person who grew up in extreme poverty said to me, "Growing up in poverty is like growing up in a foreign country. No one explains to you what you do know, what you do not know, or what you could know."

2. The resource base of themselves or other individuals used to negotiate an environment in order to know which interventions to use

Many professionals think poverty and wealth are related to money. They actually are much more related to a set of resources to which one has access. Interventions work because the resources are there to make them work. If that basic concept is not understood, then any intervention will not be successful. For example, if a parent cannot read (mental resource), then there is no success in asking the parent to read to the child.

3. The basic patterns in the mindset differences between classes so that one can have social bridging capital

In order to relate to someone different than you, there must be enough understanding of that person's reality to have a conversation. The "hidden rules" allow you to understand that there may be different thinking than yours. Members of a group that has the most people (dominant culture), the most money, or the most power tend to believe that their "hidden rules" are the best. In fact, hidden rules are often equated with intelligence. Knowing different sets of hidden rules allows one to negotiate more environments successfully. "Social bridging capital" (Putnam, 2000) are individuals you know who are different than you because they can impact your thinking if there is mutual respect. As we say to audiences, "Social bonding capital helps you get by, social bridging capital helps you get ahead."

4. The key issues in transition

A huge issue for the secondary students and adults with whom we work is transition. If individuals desire to be better educated, make a change in their living situation, end addiction, have better health, or have a better job, then what is it that those individuals need to know in order to do that? We find that they must assess and develop a resource base, develop social bridging relationships, have a language to talk about their own experience and the one they are moving to, and live in a "decontextualized" world of paper/computers. The book provides the understandings and tools to do this.

5. Key issues in the intergenerational transfer of knowledge

Part of human capital is a knowledge base. Knowledge bases are a form of privilege, just as social access and money are. Such knowledge bases also can be passed on intergenerationally. In an Australian study, which followed 8,556 children for 14 years, the researchers found they could predict with reasonable accuracy the verbal reasoning scores of 14-year-olds based on

Readings

the maternal grandfather's occupation (Najman et al., 2004).

Part of the intergenerational transfer of knowledge is also vocabulary. Hart and Risley (1995) put tape recorders in homes by economic class and recorded the language that children have access to between the ages of 1 and 3. They found that a 3-year-old in a professional household has a larger vocabulary than an adult in a welfare household. In fact, by age 4, children in welfare households had heard 13 million words compared with 45 million words in a professional household. Vocabulary is key in negotiating situations and environments.

6. **The abstract representational skills and procedural planning skills that one has to have in order to go from the situated learning of poverty to the decontextualized environment of formal schooling**

Lave & Wenger (1991) indicate that beginning learning is always about a "situated environment" that has "people, relationships, context, tasks and language." They add that when an individual makes the transition to formal schooling, learning becomes decontextualized. The context is taken away, relationships are not considered in the learning, reasoning is not with stories but with laws and symbols (abstract representational systems). The research indicates that to make the transition between those two environments, one needs relationships and support systems.

Furthermore, in a study released in 2008 using EEG scans with poor and middle-class children, the researchers found that the prefrontal cortex of the brain (executive function) in poor children was undeveloped and resembled the brains of adults who have had strokes. The executive function of the brain handles impulse control, planning, and working memory (Kishiyama, Boyce, Jimenez, Perry, & Knight, in press, p. 1). The researchers went on to state that it is remediable, but there must be direct interven-

tion. So teaching planning is critical for success in the decontextualized environment of school because it is not taught in the environment of generational poverty.

The book provides the tools to assist with this transition.

7. **The necessity of relationships of mutual respect in learning**

All learning is double coded—emotionally and cognitively (Greenspan & Benderly, 1997). The nature of the relationship makes a huge difference in how the information is coded emotionally and therefore received. In a study of 910 first-graders, even when the pedagogy of both teachers was excellent, at-risk students would not learn from a teacher if the student perceived the teacher as being "cold and uncaring" (Goleman, 1995).

In short, *Framework* provides the tools to give choice to people who do not want to live in poverty. It provides the tools for practitioners themselves to relate, reframe, and repeat.

Why do so many critics love to hate it?

In the last five years, critics have attacked the work, and almost all are connected with higher education in some manner (adjunct faculty, assistant professors, et al.). A large part of it appears to have to do with the nature of the role.

First of all, researchers ask questions and must have a clean methodology in order to publish. Researchers need to publish in order to get tenure and to keep their job. You cannot publish if your methodology is not clean, your details are not perfect, all the qualifiers are not included, and your definitions are not exact. Researchers are trained to critique ideas, details, theory, methodology, and findings but not to assess the practicality of the suggestions or situations. Furthermore, many researchers believe that "researched" information has much more value than information acquired through "practice." In fact, Bohn (2006) asks, "How had someone so widely hailed in the public schools as an expert on poverty been ignored by national research institutes, higher education, and all the major, published authorities on the subject of poverty?" In other words, the information does not have value because it has not been acknowledged by higher education.

Practitioners, on the other hand, must have solutions to practical problems. Working with people involves a messy social ecology. To keep your job you must handle and solve problems quickly. If you are a teacher in a classroom with 30 students, then details are not the focus, patterns are; methodology is not considered; group well-being ensures safety of individuals; and the focus is on working with each student for high achievement results. Furthermore, there is simply not the time to document all the details or identify the theoretical frames of the situation. Practitioners deal with people and situations and must have a level of understanding about them in order to meet their needs. Change is one of the agendas of practitioners, so efforts focus on that as well.

Why do critics love to hate the work? Quite simply, the work breaks the rules of higher education around the issue of credibility.

1. *It does not document every detail with the source* (Bomer, Dworin, May, & Semingson, 2008).
2. *It does not explain the information with details and qualifiers but rather in patterns or stereotyping* (Bohn, 2006; Bomer et al., 2008; Gorski, 2005).
3. *It does not reference systems issues or exploitation issues or racial or gender information and their roles in poverty. It does not address the macro-level issues* (Bohn, 2006; Bomer et al., 2008; Gorski, 2005).

4. *It does not have a clean methodology. It has a mixed methodology.*
5. *It looks at what students cannot do and what needs to be taught—deficit model* (Bomer et al., 2008; Gorski, 2005).
6. *It can be misused and misunderstood, so therefore it is dangerous* (Bohn, 2006).
7. *The writer self-published. The book is not peer-reviewed.* (It could be argued that selling 1.4 million copies is a form of peer review.)
8. *Race and class are not talked about together. Therefore, the work is racist* (Gorski, 2005). (As an aside, the book does not discuss gender and class either, and poverty tends to be feminized around the world.)

What seems to be an additional outrage in the criticism is the number of books that have been sold; almost every critic mentions it. Rather than asking why so many people would find the information helpful, the critics belittle the readers as not having enough intelligence to know their own biases (Bohn, 2006; Bomer et al., 2008; Gorski, 2005).

In defense of higher education, however, there is not a good research methodology for social ecologies. Neither quantitative nor qualitative methods address social ecologies very well. Norretranders (1991) explains that the research in entropy leads to the understandings of information technology. Perhaps fractal or chaos theory would provide a better theoretical model for researching social ecologies.

Does it work? Does it help make changes? Does it build human capital?

Unequivocally, yes. In some places more so than other places that use the work. Implementation is always messy and uneven. We have collected research against a set of fidelity instruments for more than seven years in K–12 settings; these data have been compiled by Dr. William Swan and peer reviewed ("Scientific Research Based Results," 2009).

A few key findings were ...

When using the normal distribution to determine expected frequencies and analyzing the observed versus the expected frequencies: In mathematics, there were twice as many positive findings as would be expected in a normal distribution (statistically significant at the .05 level); in literacy/language arts, there were three times as many positive results as would be expected in a normal distribution (statistically significant at the .001 level).

- These results led Swan to conclude, "The large number of statistically significant findings for the Payne School Model strongly supports the efficacy of the Model in improving student achievement in mathematics and English/reading/literacy/language arts."

- Additionally, an external review of nine research reports on the Payne School Model, led by Dr. C. Thomas Holmes (n.d.), professor at the University of Georgia, was completed. Holmes, along with four other reviewers, concluded that the design employed in these studies was appropriate, the statistical tests were well-chosen and clearly reported, and the author's conclusions followed directly from the obtained results.

We also have hard data about the impact on adults as well. Using *Getting Ahead in a Just-Gettin'-By World* by Phil DeVol, using concepts and tools in *Framework*, we are seeing phenomenal results. YWCA National named "Bridges out of Poverty/Getting Ahead" as a model program in December 2008. These are the results that the YWCA of Saint Joseph County, IN, is getting.

Increase in participants:	Positive change in 3 months	Positive changes in 6 months
Income	26%	84%
Education	36%	69%
Employment	32%	63%
Support Systems	13%	84%

Conclusion

The book is about developing human capital through relationships and education at the micro level.

I am baffled why the discussion so often must be polarized; in other words, if one idea is right, then another idea must be wrong. Poverty is multifaceted. In fact, the subject is analogous to the six blind men and the elephant. If we are ever going to successfully address poverty, it will take all the ideas, as well as greater understandings than we have at present.

References

Bohn, A. (2006). Rethinking schools online: A framework for understanding Ruby Payne. Retrieved April 27, 2009, from www.rethinkingschools.org/archive/21_02/fram212.shtml

Bomer, R., Dworin, J., May, L., & Semingson, P. (2008). Miseducating teachers about the poor: A critical analysis of Ruby Payne's claims about poverty. *Teachers College Record, 110,* 2497–2531.

DeVol, P. E. (2004). *Getting ahead in a just-gettin'-by world: Building your resources for a better life* (2nd ed.). Highlands, TX: aha! Process.

Deutschman, A. (2007). *Change or die: The three keys to change at work and in life.* New York, NY: HarperCollins.

Goleman, D. (1995). *Emotional intelligence: Why it can matter more than IQ.* New York, NY: Bantam Books.

Gorski, P. (2005). *Savage unrealities: Uncovering classism in Ruby Payne's framework* [Abridged version]. Retrieved April 27, 2009, from http://www.edchange.org/publications/Savage_Unrealities_abridged.pdf

Greenspan, S. I., & Benderly, B. L. (1997). *The growth of the mind and the endangered origins of intelligence.* Reading, MA: Addison-Wesley.

Hart, B., & Risley, T. R. (1995). *Meaningful differences in the everyday experience of young American children.* Baltimore: Paul H. Brookes.

Holmes, C. T. (n.d.). Review of program evaluations. Retrieved April 27, 2009, from http://www.ahaprocess.com/files/R&D_School/ExternalReviewRevised.pdf

Isaacs, J. B., Sawhill, I. V., & Haskins, R. (n.d.). Getting ahead or losing ground: Economic Mobility in America. Retrieved April 27, 2009, from http://www.pewtrusts.org/uploadedFiles/wwwpewtrustsorg/Reports/Economic_Mobility/Economic_Mobility_in_America_Full.pdf

Kishiyama, M. M., Boyce, W. T., Jimenez, A. M., Perry, L. M., & Knight, R. T. (in press). Socioeconomic disparities affect prefrontal function in children. *Journal of Cognitive Neuroscience.* Available from http://www.mitpressjournals.org/doi/abs/10.1162/jocn.2009.21101

Lave, J., & Wenger, E. (1991). *Situated learning: Legitimate peripheral participation.* Cambridge, England: Cambridge University Press.

Najman, J. M., Aird, R., Bor, W., O'Callaghan, M., Williams, G., & Shuttlewood, G. (2004). The generational transmission of socioeconomic inequalities in child cognitive development and emotional health. *Social Science and Medicine, 58,* 1147–1158.

Norretranders, T. (1991). *The user illusion: Cutting consciousness down to size.* New York, NY: Penguin.

Payne, R. K. (2005). *A framework for understanding poverty* (4th ed.). Highlands, TX: aha! Process.

Putnam, R. D. (2000). *Bowling alone: The collapse and revival of American community.* New York, NY: Simon & Schuster.

Scientific research based results of aha! Process. (2009). Retrieved April 27, 2009, from http://www.ahaprocess.com/School_Programs/Research_&_Development/Scientific_Research.html

Note. From *From Understanding Poverty to Building Human Capacity,* by Ruby K. Payne, 2012.

Bibliography

Berger, K. S. (2010). *The developing person through the life span* (8th ed.). New York, NY: Worth Publishers.

Berliner, D. C. (1988, October). Implications of studies of expertise in pedagogy for teacher education and evaluation. Paper presented at Educational Testing Service Invitational Conference on New Directions for Teacher Assessment. New York, NY.

Berliner, D. C. (2009). *Poverty and potential: Out of school factors and school success.* Boulder, CO: National Educational Policy Center. Retrieved from http://epicpolicy.org/publication/povertyand-potential.

Berne, E. (1996). *Games people play: The basic handbook of transactional analysis.* New York, NY: Ballantine Books.

Bloom, B. (1976). *Human characteristics and school learning.* New York, NY: McGraw-Hill.

Caine, R. N., & Caine, G. (1991). *Making connections: Teaching and the human brain.* Alexandria, VA: Association for Supervision and Curriculum Development.

Collins, B. C. (1997). *Emotional unavailability: Recognizing it, understanding it, and avoiding its trap.* Lincolnwood, IL: NTC/Contemporary Publishing Co.

Covey, S. R. (1989). *The 7 habits of highly effective people: Powerful lessons in personal change.* New York, NY: Simon & Schuster.

DeVol, P. E. (2004). *Getting ahead in a just-gettin'-by world: Building your resources for a better life* (2nd ed.). Highlands, TX: aha! Process.

Feuerstein, R., et al. (1980). *Instrumental enrichment: An intervention program for cognitive modifiability.* Glenview, IL: Scott, Foresman & Co.

Forbes 400 richest Americans. (2011). New York, NY: Forbes.com LLC. Retrieved from http://www.forbes.com/wealth/forbes-400

Gladwell, M. (2005). *Blink: The power of thinking without thinking.* New York, NY: Little, Brown.

Hart, B., & Risley, T. R. (1995). *Meaningful differences in the everyday experience of young American children.* Baltimore, MD: P. H. Brookes.

Idol, L., & Jones, B. F. (Eds.). (1991). *Educational values and cognitive instruction: Implications for reform.* Mahwah, NJ: Erlbaum.

Isaacs, J. B. (2007). Economic mobility across generations. Economic Mobility Project, Pew Charitable Trusts. Retrieved from http://www. pewtrusts.org/uploadedFiles/wwwpewtrustsorg/Reports/Economic_Mobility/EMP%20Across%20Generations%20ES%20+%20Chapter.Pdf

Jones, B. F., Pierce, J., & Hunter, B. (1988). Teaching students to construct graphic representations. *Educational Leadership, 46*(4), 20–25.

Joos, M. (1967). The styles of the five clocks. In R. D. Abraham & R. C. Troike (Eds.), *Language and cultural diversity in American education* (pp. 145–149). Englewood Cliffs, NJ: Prentice Hall.

Marzano, R. J., & Arredondo, D. (1986). *Tactics for thinking.* Aurora, CO: Mid-Continent Regional Educational Laboratory.

Najman, J. M., Aird, R., Bor, W., O'Callaghan, M., Williams, G. M., & Shuttlewood, G. J. (2004). The generational transmission of socioeconomic inequalities in child cognitive development and emotional health. *Social Science and Medicine, 58*(6), 1147–1158. doi:10.1016/S0277-9536(03)00286-7

Palincsar, A. S., & Brown, A. L. (1984). The reciprocal teaching of comprehension-fostering and comprehension-monitoring activities. *Cognition and Instruction, 1*(2). 117–175.

Payne, R. K. (1996). Working with students from poverty: Discipline. *Instructional Leader,* Texas Elementary Principals and Supervisors Association.

Payne, R. K. (2004). No child left behind, part IV: Parent and community involvement. *Instructional Leader, 17*(6), 1–2, 9–12. Retrieved from http://www.tepsa.org/associations/9767/files/Publications/ILSampleRubyPayne4.pdf

Payne, R. K. (2005). *Crossing the tracks for love: What to do when you and your partner grew up in different worlds.* Highlands, TX: aha! Process.

Payne, R. K. (2006). *Working with parents: Building relationships for student success.* Highlands, TX: aha! Process.

Payne, R. K. (2009). *Research-based strategies: Narrowing the achievement gap for under-resourced learners.* Highlands, TX: aha! Process.

Payne, R. K. (2012). *From understanding poverty to building human capacity: Ruby Payne's articles on transforming individuals, families, schools, churches, and communities.* Highlands, TX: aha! Process.

Sharron, H., & Coulter, M. (1994). *Changing children's minds: Feuerstein's revolution in the teaching of intelligence.* Exeter, Great Britain: BPC Wheatons Ltd.

TESA (Teacher Expectations & Student Achievement), Los Angeles Department of Education. Los Angeles, CA.

Wolin, S. J., & Wolin, S. (1994). *The resilient self: How survivors of troubled families rise above adversity.* New York, NY: Villard Books.

U.S. Bureau of the Census. (2000). www.census.gov

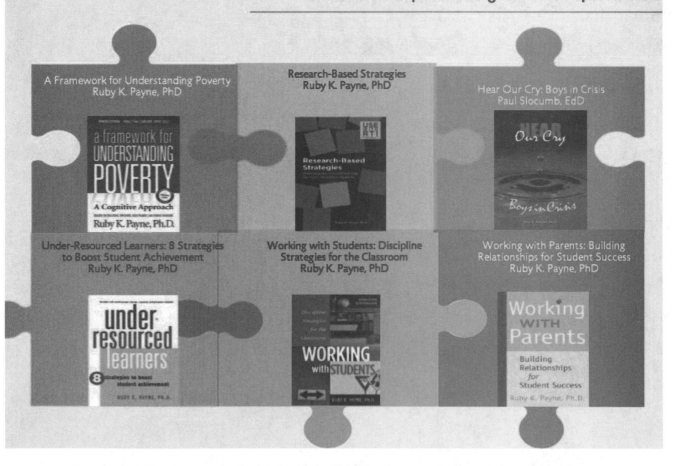

WE'D LIKE TO HEAR FROM YOU!

 **Join us on Facebook**
www.facebook.com/rubypayne

 **Respond to our blog**
www.ahaprocess.com/blog

 **Subscribe to our YouTube channel**
www.youtube.com/ahaprocess

 **Download free resources**
www.ahaprocess.com

Visit our online store for related titles by Dr. Payne

- *Research-Based Strategies: Narrowing the Achievement Gap for Under-Resourced Learners*
- *School Improvement: 9 Systemic Processes to Raise Achievement* (Payne & Magee)
- *From Understanding Poverty to Building Human Capacity: Ruby Payne's Articles on Transforming Individuals, Families, Schools, Churches, and Communities*
- *Working with Students: Discipline Strategies for the Classroom*
- *Removing the Mask: How to Identify and Develop Giftedness in Students from Poverty* (Payne & Slocumb)

Download an eBook

Sign up for a one-hour SHORT COURSE online

Articles

What Information Does A Framework for Understanding Poverty Have That Cannot Be Obtained Easily from Other Sources? Why Do Critics Love to Hate It and Practitioners Love to Use It? (Payne) http://www.ahaprocess.com/wp-content/uploads/2013/08/Framework-for-Understanding-Poverty-Info-Not-Easily-Obtained-Elsewhere.pdf

"Neighborhood Effects" (Payne)
https://www.ahaprocess.com/wp-content/uploads/2014/10/Neighborhood-Effects-and-Poverty.pdf

Social Risk Factors through the Triple Lens (Payne & DeVol)
https://www.ahaprocess.com/wp-content/uploads/2014/10/Risk-Factors-Through-Triple-Lens.pdf

"12 Thinking tools for Bridges Out of Poverty Initiatives" (Devol)
http://www.ahaprocess.com/wp-content/uploads/2014/04/12-Thinking-Tools-for-Bridges-Initiatives.pdf

"Starting a Bridges Community" [video] (DeVol)
http://youtu.be/uJHeMGvlTAM

5-Point stability scale (indicators with 5 indicators per category), Getting Ahead in a Just-Gettin'-By World (DeVol)
https://www.ahaprocess.com/wp-content/uploads/2014/10/Stability-Scale-Indicators.pdf

The Policy Paper on Education: "How Do We Create Intellectual Capital (Talent and Expertise) on a Mass Scale" (Payne)
https://www.ahaprocess.com/wp-content/uploads/2014/10/How-Do-We-Create-Intellectual-Capital.pdf

Publications

 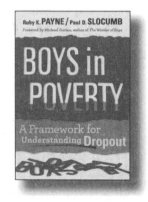 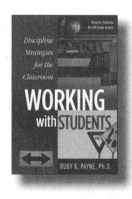 

  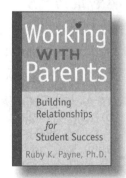 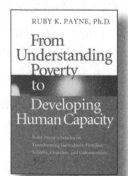

www.ahaprocess.com